ODD COUPLES

FROM THE HISTORY OF CINEMA

Jean-Luc Godard: The Passion of Cinema / Le Passion de Cinéma
by Jeremy Mark Robinson

Julia Kristeva: Art, Love, Melancholy, Philosophy, Semiotics
by Kelly Ives

Luce Irigaray: Lips, Kissing, and the Politics of Sexual Difference
by Kelly Ives

Helene Cixous I Love You: The Jouissance *of Writing*
by Kelly Ives

MEDIA, FEMINISM, CULTURAL STUDIES

Marvelous Names
by P. Adams Sitney

Stepping Forward: Essays, Lectures and Interviews
by Wolfgang Iser

Liv Tyler
by Thomas A. Christie

The Cinema of Richard Linklater
by Thomas A. Christie

Walerian Borowczyk
by Jeremy Mark Robinson

Wild Zones: Pornography, Art and Feminism
by Kelly Ives

'Cosmo Woman': The World of Women's Magazines
by Oliver Whitehorne

Andrea Dworkin
by Jeremy Mark Robinson

Cixous, Irigaray, Kristeva: The Jouissance of French Feminism
by Kelly Ives

Sex in Art: Pornography and Pleasure in Painting and Sculpture
by Cassidy Hughes

The Erotic Object: Sexuality in Sculpture
From Prehistory to the Present Day
by Susan Quinnell

Women in Pop Music
by Helen Challis

Detonation Britain: Nuclear War in the UK
by Jeremy Mark Robinson

The Sacred Cinema of Andrei Tarkovsky
by Jeremy Mark Robinson

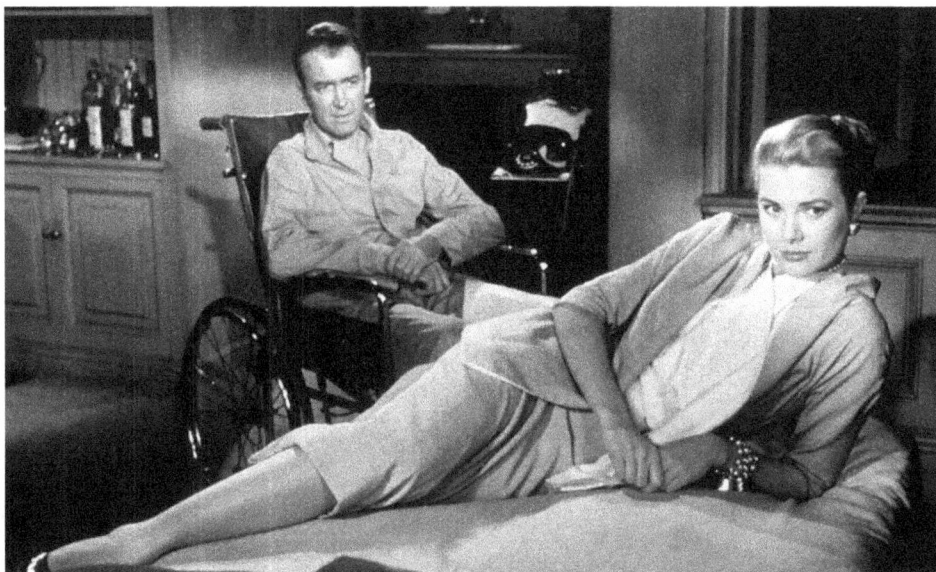

ODD COUPLES

from the history of cinema

P. ADAMS SITNEY

Crescent Moon

Crescent Moon Publishing
P.O. Box 1312, Maidstone
Kent, ME14 5XU, Great Britain
www.crmoon.com

First published 2025.
© P. Adams Sitney 2025.

Set in Book Antiqua 10 on 14pt.
Designed by Radiance Graphics.

British Library Cataloguing in Publication data available for this title.

I.S.B.N.-13 9781861712448
I.S.B.N.-13 9781861714268

CONTENTS

Mirror (1974).

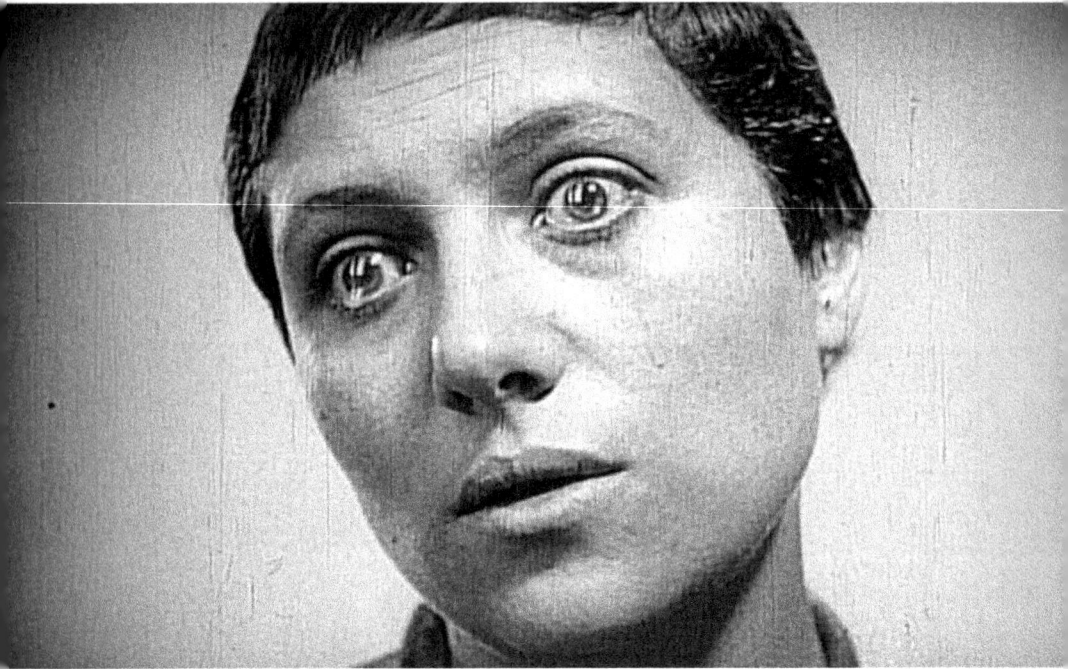

The Passion of Joan of Arc (1928).

Acknowledgements

The original working title for this book was *Incongruous Pairings from the History of Cinema*. Jeremy Robinson, my editor and publisher at Crescent Moon Publishing picked *Odd Couples* which I enlarged with the phrase "from the History of Cinema." The book itself grew out of my final lecture (of five) at the Cinemateca portuguesa in June 2023: I had planned to show and interpret *Persona*, but it was not available. So, when I screened Tarkovsky's *The Mirror* instead, I realized that its affinities to Bergman's film were much greater than I had previously thought. Once I returned to Rhode Island, and wrote out the lecture, I recalled first the relation of Bergman's *Smiles of a Summer's Night* to Dreyer's *Vredens Dag*, then I understood that I had lectured on several unexpected couplings from my courses on film history at Princeton University. I had been thinking about many of these pairs for decades; so the chapters coupling them incorporate several short texts I had previously written: on Saul Levine, Morgan Fisher, George Landow and Peter Hutton for *Artforum*; Greenaway's *The Falls* for *Persistence of Vision*; Antonioni's *The Red Desert* for *The Psychoanalytic Review*; Mekas's *Birth of a Nation* for *Images Are Real*; the essays on Kelman for *Logos* and Cavell for *Conversations*; the text on Marjorie Keller first appeared as the Introduction to the Spanish translation of her book, *The Untutored Eye*; only the combination of Scorsese's *The Last Temptation of Christ* and Allen's *Crimes and Misdemeanors* had appeared coupled as such previously, in *Raritan*. I had also lectured on Hollis Frampton for the Room East Gallery in New York, and *There's Something About Mary* at Anthology Film Archives. The transcriptions of those lectures aided me in writing the relevant part-chapters. All of these texts were altered for this book, some thoroughly, some hardly at all.

When Light Industry invited me to introduce Gregory Markopoulos's *Lysis* and *Charmides*, the uncertain recognition of figure of Persephone in the former film recalled my interpretation of Hitchcock's *Vertigo*, giving me a penultimate (but not chronologically late) entry. Finally, I used David Lynch's *Blue Velvet* with two very different pairings.

Sources

Most of the interview in the Epilogue initially appeared as "Film/ Religion: A Conversation with P. Adams Sitney," by Sérgio Dias Branco, *Cinema: Journal of Philosophy and the Moving Image,* no. 4.

The bibliographic details of the previously published texts follow:

"Cinematic Election and Theological Vanity," *Raritan,* vol. 11, no. 2, Fall 1991, pp. 48-65.

"*The Falls,*" *Persistence of Vision* no. 8, 1990.

"*Il Deserto Rosso,*" in *The Psychoanalytic Review*, vol. 105, no. 5 (October 2018), pp. 555-565.

"Medium Shots: The Films of Morgan Fisher," *Artforum,* January 2006, pp. 200-205.

"Immanent Domain: The Films of Peter Hutton," *Artforum,* October, 2008, pp. 135-140.

"Taking Note: On the Films of Saul Levine" *Artforum,* May, 2007, pp. 350-55.

"Passages (Owen Land)," *Artforum*, November 2011, pp. 63-66

"Apologies to Stanley Cavell" in *Conversations 7: The Journal of Cavellian Studies 7* (2019), pp. 8-13.

Logos (vol. 22, no. 3 (2023): https://logosjournal.com/2023/on-ken-kelman-and-his-theoryof-cinema/): "Introduction" to Ken

Kelman, *Lectures and Essay* (forthcoming from Anthology Film Archives)

"Film/ Religion: A Conversation with P. Adams Sitney," by Sérgio Dias Branco, *Cinema: Journal of Philosophy and the Moving Image no. 4*, (2013) pp. 210-214

"Watching *Birth of a Nation*" appeared in *Jonas Mekas - Images are Real*, curated by Francesco Urbano Ragazzi, at Mattatoio. Roma, 2023, pp. 34-41

The text on Marjorie Keller first appeared in Spanish Translation as the Preface to her book *Un Ojo Sin Adoctrinar*, translated by Paula Camacho Rodán (Sevilla, Cine Authentica, 2022).

Most of the section on Hollis Frampton was delivered at the Room East Gallery and posted online as http:// www.roomeast.com/wordpress/wp-content/uploads/2015/10/P-ADAMS-SITNEY-LECTURE-FINAL.pdf.

I owe a great debt to my agent George Borchardt, Inc. (and his employees) who has stuck with me for decades, and at least seven books, for a mere pittance.

Publisher's Note: This book was completed by P. Adams Sitney several months before he died in June, 2025.

Chaplin
and
La Passion de Jeanne d'Arc [The Passion of Joan of Arc]

What constitutes the center of the silent screen? For Charles Chaplin the screen is a rectangle; he put his tramp figure in the center of the screen, often filmed frontally, or used his framing and gestures to make him the center of attention. Carl Theodor Dreyer, having conceived of the cinematic locus as a circle, used an elaborate range of camera gestures to make Joan occupy the center of his film *La Passion de Jeanne d'Arc* [*The Passion of Joan of Arc*] (1929).

In *The Gold Rush* (1925) the tramp-prospector demonstrates his ecstasy when Georgia, the dance-hall girl on whom he dotes, insincerely agrees to come to New Year's Eve dinner at his cabin by a displaced or symbolic masturbation. At the climax of an acrobatic display, he whacks his pillow so hard that feathers explode orgasmically all over the screen image and he wiggles his worn-out, fire-charred shoes in delight. The scene is all the funnier because Georgia who forgot her gloves, returned to the cabin to witness the Tramp's enthusiastic excesses. She and her three "dance hall" companions never come to dinner, although the Tramp had elaborately prepared a roast and a candle-lit table with Christmas presents for all four prostitutes, while unbeknownst to him they are still dancing with big, handsome men at the "Dance Hall."

After fighting off a mule who shows up instead, he dozes at the table, dreaming of the successful party where he shows off the Ocean Roll Dance, with rolls on the ends of two forks. With Orphic aplomb, Chaplin set the camera close to his face, as he brilliantly manipulated the forked rolls as if they were feet of a chorus girl. At the same time, he mimed the deadpan expressions of the female dancer. In an act of self-congratulation at this tour-de-force the applauding hands of the guests can be seen clapping at the edge of the film frame, and the title card, "He's wonderful" follows. A kiss from Georgia knocks him out, as the image of him asleep at the table fades to a clock showing midnight. When the Tramp goes in search of his absent guests, Georgia conceives of a gag: she will bring the three friends and her lover, Jack, armed with a pistol to scare the tramp. But when she finds the vestiges of his spoiled party, she declared, "The joke has gone too far," and rejects Jack and his long pistol in favor of the more imaginative suitor. Thus, the mild-mannered, excessively polite Tramp has won the audience's sympathy yet again. He is an ideal lover who deservedly strikes it rich in the gold fields; Georgia has earned her own livelihood and represents "the good-hearted prostitute," truly in love with tramp. On the ship taking them back home, she offers to pay his fare when she mistakes him for a stowaway after he falls onto the second-class deck in a photoshoot. Evidentially Chaplin put this development into the film to prove that she is not after him for his wealth.

The supreme instance of the Tramp's goodness would be the more ambiguous ending of *City Lights* (1931). He has fallen in love with a beautiful, blind flower seller who takes him for a gentleman. A wealthy drunk has also taken a liking to him. Ultimately, he robs the drunk to finance an operation to restore the woman's sight. After he is released from prison for his theft, he happens upon the spot where she used to sell flowers. (Now she and her mother operate their own flower shop nearby.) The tramp dominates almost every shot of the finale, except a brief exchange between the woman and a rich young man whom she pathetically mistakes for her benefactor, and the newsboys who previously taunted the Tramp at that spot, loading a peashooter to discharge at him.

Even in the shot of his recognition of the woman, his image is paramount. She is in the foreground inside the shop, laughing at his reaction to the teasing newsboys when he notices her through the shop window. Her response to him is even crueler than that of the boys. She tells her mother, "I seem to have made a conquest," as she prepares to give him a coin and to replace the discarded flower in his lapel with a fresh one. When she cannot entice him into the shop, she pursues him outside. As soon as she touches his hand to press the coin upon him, she realizes from the touch who he is. The title card "You?" underlines the pathos of the scene. He barely nods, saying "You can see now?" After her lips move, we read, "Yes, I can see now." before the film ends on the Tramp's smiling face, with one finger in his mouth as he holds the white rose she gave him. Her shock and disappointment are as palpable as his joy. Despite the Ocean Roll Dance or the whole of *The Gold Rush*, the end of *City Lights* is Chaplin's greatest cinematic achievement. It needs no image of applause or a kiss. With utter confidence in his mimetic skills, and superbly directing the woman (or children) who refract those skills, he has placed himself in the center of his shots.

In *La Passion de Jeanne d'Arc* Dreyer has used camera movement and blocking to put Joan at the virtual center of his film. The publication of an historical transcript of Joan's trial, in the 1840s, provided the filmmaker with the basis of his work. It is a deliberately silent film, made as sound cinema was being introduced in the United States. Dreyer emphasized the role of speech in this drama by using the French title cards to interrupt the speeches of Joan and her interrogators so that we can lip-read what they are saying. The title cards interrupt the mouthing of questions and responses from the trial record as the speaker begins with his or her lip movement; it continues after the reading. Joan's answers in her defense are often astonishingly brilliant. Only the sympathetic monk, Jean Massieu (played by Antonin Artaud) takes her side. With brilliant blocking Dreyer's ecclesiastical interrogators surround Jeanne. The moving camera pans around the virtual circumference they form, occasionally shooting along a radius to and from Jeanne. The circular motion is reflected in the spinning torture wheel and even in the 360-degree rotation of the outdoor camera when she is at the stake.

The film seems to restate the theological idea that "God is a circle whose center is everywhere and whose circumference is nowhere." The phrase has been attributed to Empedocles, Augustine, and Nicolas of Cusa and was cited frequently by Voltaire, Otto, and Jung. The film's title and several images suggest that Jeanne's passion (suffering) is an *imitatio Christi*: although she is tried by intellectual superiors, her wise responses are to no avail; she is imprisoned, tortured, mocked by her jailers, and executed. Where Chaplin counted on his own supreme mimetic skill and multiple film takes to make his Tramp the nearly divine center of his films, Dreyer endowed his actress, Renée Jeanne Falconetti, with a similar aura, by refusing to allow her to wear makeup, cutting off her hair on screen, and other reputedly sadistic strategies. As with Chaplin, reshooting scenes was essential to Dreyer's perfectionism. He watched initial takes with Falconetti and then repeated the shots to emphasize details he liked. Thus, Chaplin and Falconetti were the probably greatest male and female performers of the silent cinema.

Un chien andalou [An Andalusian Dog]
and
Blue Velvet

David Lynch shared Luis Buñuel's and Salvador Dalí's fascination with what had been considered entomology; ants appear prominently in *Un chien andalou* [*An Andalusian Dog*, 1929] and *L'age d'or* starts off as if it were a documentary on scorpions. *Blue Velvet* (1986) begins in the grass with insects and its narrative takes off from the moment "Jeffery" finds a severed ear in a field, after suspending college to look after his father, stricken with a stroke or heart attack.

Both Kenneth Anger's *Scorpio Rising* (1963) and Alfred Hitchcock's *Rear Window* (1954) had a greater direct influence on the film; the former introduced Bobby Vinton's 1963 song (created by Bernie Wayne and Lee Morris in 1950) to cinema, while the latter gave Jeffrey his name and his penchant for erotic espionage. (Dorothy's name seems to be an homage to *The Wizard of Oz* [1939], another crucial film for Lynch's art.)

Un chien andalou is a remarkably violent film. Early on we see a man, played by Buñuel himself, slice open the eye of the female lead, although in the ensuing film both her eyes are intact. The cinematic illusionism of the scene is undercut by the shot of the vitreous fluid flowing out of an animal's eye. Later a potential source for the shot is revealed when two dead donkeys appear inside a grand piano, with gore streaming from their eyes. Likewise, a close shot of ants crawling out of a hole in the male protagonist's hand turns out to be a trick from the very same prop that the filmmakers used when a hand is severed in a later automobile accident. First, Buñuel and Dalí create a shockingly violent illusion and then, in a later uncanny image of further violence, reveal how it was manufactured. Lynch seems to have no interest in unmasking cinematic illusionism although he twists his plot by putting the drug-dealing sadist, Frank Booth, in a mask, as if he were a different character, to deceive the viewers for most of the film. (The temporary deception of viewers, and the eventual revelation of the viewer's error, is a stock element of the mystery or detective film genre.) Generally, Lynch exploits the sexual undertones of *Rear Window* by making them explicit, and by portraying Dorothy as a masochist, Jeffrey as a voyeur, and Frank Booth and his gang as sadists.

Un chien andalou was originally entitled with the warning commonly found on trains: "It is dangerous to lean out the window." But Federico García Lorca insisted that the tile of the released film was an insult to him, as an impotent, Andalusian homosexual; Buñuel denied that. The protagonist of the film, whom García Lorca took for a satire on himself, is stimulated by pain and horror. When he sees the accident through a second story window, he sexually attacks and molests the female lead. Defending herself, she painfully pins his arm by closing a door on it. That is when the ants crawl out of his palm, in a displacement of masturbation that precedes a parallel act in *L'Age d'or*.

Blue Velvet has its own intimations of impotence and sexual frustration: in the opening sequence, while Jeffrey's nearly catatonic mother watches a big pistol on television, his father twists the hose with which he is trying to water the lawn, so that almost nothing comes out while he collapses with a neck pain and a small dog drinks the water freely flowing from the hose, held at crotch level.

Later, when Dorothy catches Jeffrey peeping at her and Frank through the slats of her closet door, she fellates him and forces him to have sex with her. Frank Booth has a ritual for sexual satisfaction: he habitually breaths in oxygen; he punches Dorothy if she looks at him: he examines her vagina and takes the belt of her blue velvet robe in his mouth; she has to talk to him as if he were her infant child. When he finds Jeffrey in her apartment, he seizes him, taking him to Ben's bordello where Dean Stockwell, as Ben, plays a stage homosexual, singing Karaoke, before Frank's gang beat up Jeffrey, after Frank, putting messy lipstick on himself between hits of oxygen, kisses him on the mouth. What Buñuel and Dalí's film suggests through symbolism, Lynch presents more or less realistically.

The story of Frank Booth and Dorothy Vallens gradually builds to a climactic murder and escape scene, then Lynch moves to an uncanny epilogue that recapitulates several of the images that opening the film: after an ominous closeup on Jeffrey's ear, we see a white picket fence with red and yellow roses, and the local fire engine parading in slow motion through the small Southern town; only now Dorothy Vallens has her son restored to her (Booth had kidnapped him and murdered her husband) and the parents of Sandy and Jeffrey are about to share a barbeque, but a blatantly mechanical robin (an iconic image of Love according to Sandy), is eating an insect, to the horror of Jeffrey's aunt, who resembles a bug herself. *Blue Velvet* attempted to lift the curtain on the façade of "happy" smalltown America.

Un chien andalou, more radically, depicted the unconscious violence and uncanniness of eros: it too concludes with a curious diminuendo: After a parody of shot-countershot ends the struggles of the protagonist, who he wipes away his mouth as the woman puts on makeup and lipstick. When pubic hair appears where his mouth had been, she sticks out her tongue at him and looks to find her underarm hair gone. Then she steps out of the second-story urban apartment onto a windy beach, where a lover silently reproves her lateness. They kiss and stroll along the beach, apparently reconciled, finding and contemptuously discarding washed-up paraphernalia from the earlier part of the film. An intertitle, "Au Printemps" [In the Spring] introduces their two figures half-buried in the beach sand, presumably dead. The box and rope they found in their stroll corresponds to the closeup of Jeffrey's ear in *Blue Velvet*. Both films stress the cyclical recurrence of profound disturbances underlying the mythos of Romantic Love.

L'Age d'or [The Golden Age]
and
Vampyr

Two early sound films, the first made by their directors, mark the transition from the silent cinema with extraordinary inventiveness (as if the directors had been imagining unique sound effects long before they could actually execute them.). Both Luis Buñuel's *L'Age d'or* (*The Golden Age,* 1930) and Carl Th. Dreyer's *Vampyr* (1932) make extensive use of written titles, use very little speech, and have innovative and elaborate music, as indeed *City Lights* (Chaplin's first sound film) did with the written titles.

L'Age d'or is a Surrealist social critique that mockingly calls Paris "Imperial Rome" by inserting stock footage of contemporary Italy's capitol, where a visiting relative leaves a note for the Pope stuck to a window at St. Peter's in the Vatican But for the most part, it features absurd images from Paris: a man covered in dust exiting a busy café; another man kicking a violin down a street (accompanied by violin music on the soundtrack until he stomps upon the instrument); and a man walking with a stone on his head in imitation of a statue of a stoned martyr; a series of buildings collapsing; and wind blowing out of a mirror. The action centers around the notion of the *coitus interruptus* of a couple first dragged from the mud while a ceremonial monument is dedicated on Mallorca to dead bishops killed by outlaws. The man of the couple has sadistic impulses: he breaks away from his captors to kick a small dog and to crush an insect under foot. On the street he sees a sign of a woman's legs and finger that leads him to imagine his interrupted partner masturbating. Earlier, he imagined the woman sitting on a toilet with the toilet paper beside her burning. That may have been a displaced rebus for his desire for aggressive anal intercourse. He turns out to be a diplomat invited to a fancy-dress party at her home. When he is called away from their necking for a telephone call, her frustration reaches its apex. First, she fellates the big toe of a marble statue, and then passionately kisses the elderly conductor of a rented orchestra who broke off his concert because of a migraine headache. The man, in turn, rushes to her bedroom and throws from its second-story window a priest, a heavy plow, a blowup giraffe, and the feathers from a pillow.

The feathers become the snow falling on a remote castle, where according to the intertitle a group of men had been holding a sadistic orgy for 120 days. The time frame and the events clearly allude to the recently found, unpublished manuscript of de Sade's *120 Jours de Sodom* (1785), at that time acquired by the Vicomte de Noailles who financed Buñuel's film. The Duc de Blangy emerges from the castle, looking like the traditional image of Jesus. He returns inside to a girl's scream, as if he had previously neglected to kill her. The film ends with hair pieces attached to a cross, as if displaying fetishistic totems.

The high-society partyers do not notice a servant collapsing outside a flaming kitchen, or a horse-cart conveying drunks through the house, but they gather on a balcony to watch a gamekeeper shoot and kill his son for a prank. Such violence and sadism prevail throughout the film. The opening documentary footage of scorpions, killing a rat, may be meant to suggest that humans share their natural behavior and instincts.

Just as Buñuel paid tribute to Noailles for producing *L'Age d'or*, Dreyer allowed the stolid Baron de Gunzberg to star in *Vampyr* because he paid for the independent production. He plays a nearly somnambulistic wanderer who shows up at an Inn plagued by a vampire. For international distribution, the few speaking parts were filmed in German, French, and English. Like *L'Age d'or*, *Vampyr* makes abundant use of intertitles. Along with the protagonist, Allan Gray, we read intertitles from a book about vampires to establish background information. But Dreyer seems to have had next to no interest in vampirism. His quarry is the borderline between life and death. To establish the notion of a fluid transition between those realms he included doors and windows in nearly every shot. When Gray imagines his own death and burial, even his coffin has a window through which he can still see, or be seen. Sometimes shadows become independent actors, free of the bodies that cast them.

Where Buñuel and Dalí marshalled the realism of cinema to create shocks with their surreal images, Dreyer cast his entire film in a fluid arena between life and death, dream and waking, fantasy and speculation. Even the sound seems to span the range between Wolfgang Zeller's music and voice, just as the soft-focus, gauze-filtered cinematography situates the whole film in a hazy intermediary zone between the extremes of black and white. The set designer, Hermann Warm, had previously exploited the tonalities of orthochromatic and panchromatic film stock for Weine's starkly black and white *Das Cabinet des Dr. Caligari* (1920) and the modulated tonality of Dreyer's own *La Passion de Jeanne d'Arc* (1929) by painting the castle of Jeanne's interrogation pink for a soft effect in black and white panchromatic film. Even when the sinister physician suffocates by falling into the flour of a mill, Maté's camerawork softened the brightness of the white powder. Thus, the visual texture of *Vampyr* made a strong contrast to the sharp optics of Buñuel's and Dalí's *L'age d'or* and *Un chien andalou* (1929).

Le sang d'un poète [The Blood of a Poet] and The Horse's Mouth

In this chapter I draw my incongruous pair by juxtaposing two essays by Parker Tyler. In his "Megalomaniascope and *The Horse's Mouth*" reprinted In *Sex Psyche Etcetera in the Film* (1969) the criticism of Ronald Neame's and Alec Guinness's film, based on Joyce Cary's novel of the same title (1944), is spot-on. Yet, I am still very fond of the film. They might have chosen a better painter to execute Gully Jimson's canvases than the 'Kitchen Sink' artist, John Bratby; and the script by Guinness himself might have remained more faithful to the novel. But despite these drawbacks, and others that Tyler identifies, no other film so enthusiastically expounds the glories of painting as an art.

The criticism of *The Horse's Mouth* (1958) would be a further instance of what Tyler described at least four years earlier as "The Artist Portrayed and Betrayed" in *The Three Faces of the Film* (from *Art News*, 1954) where he contrasted then recent films about artists [*Moulin Rouge* (1952), and *Rembrandt* (1935)], to Jean *Cocteau's Le sang d'un poète* (1930) (pp 52-53):

> The authenticity of an artist's imaginative world appeared much more persuasively in Cocteau's *Blood of a Poet*, where the inner

tensions of an artist's life were related to physical objects with something near the truth as verifiable through the artist's personal testimony. But Cocteau (Surrealist orthodoxy to the contrary notwithstanding) is a genuine if not always, of late, a perfectly sincere artist, and he, not another, made the film. A dazzling irony is secreted in his image of an artist who, while called a poet, is actually seen first as a painter, nude above the waist and wearing eighteenth-century breeches and white wig. Unquestionably, this costume came directly from Valentino as he appeared in a scene from the commercial film romance, *Monsieur Beaucaire* [1946] (the actor's face and hair, in addition, are much like Valentino's). Surely we have an interesting subtlety here: a film-maker who is an artist in his own right produces a convincing image of an artist by imitating the image of a screen star. Isn't Hollywood naive to assume the opposite? – that by producing the image of a screen star it imitates a convincing image of an artist?

Tyler's praise of Cocteau's film underlines how it was as underestimated in Europe (because of what it pilfered from Surrealism) and overvalued in the United States (as the fountainhead of experimental film here). He astutely observed how the homosexual Cocteau found a male fantasy ideal in popular movies. In essence, Cocteau's film is an allegory of poetic inspiration and ruthlessness, with no direct relation to the character studies to which Tyler compared it.

Gulley Jimson absorbed massive amounts of Blake's poetry in Joyce Cary's novel, and enough for it to be noticed in the film. He wanted to paint grand Blakean, Biblical themes: 'The Raising of Lazarus,' and 'The Last Judgement.' Like Cocteau's poète, he is a seer, intolerant of interruptions when the Muse is upon him; a potentially violent man, who thinks only of his art. Neame creates hilarious comedy from Jimson's irascibility, his attempts to steal from a rich collector of his early work, his disregard for the property of others, his contempt for his profession, and his obsessions, in short, from his *character*.

However, the self-destructive artist of Cocteau's film is somewhat closer to Cary's Jimson than to Guinness's version as a happy-go-lucky artist. He kills himself twice in *Le sang d'un poète*. The aging, sexless Jimson owes nothing to the poète who symbolically masturbates as a source of inspiration with the Muse's mouth on his palm, as if she were fellating him. He can magically expel intrusive visitors, as Jimson wishes to do, but comically fails when a sculptor moves in the apartment where he has been painting a wall and steals his female model as well. The events of *Le sang d'un poète* are all imaginary, but in Neame's film only Jimson's undepicted 'visions' are. None of the paintings he executes (through Bratby's brush) satisfy his inner anticipations. He has to confess that he gets pleasure only from beginning works of art.

As Tyler pointed out, there is no sense of the origins or the nature of cinema in *The Horse's Mouth*. But Cocteau's film abounds in them: after the poète plunges through a mirror, he is transported to "le hôtel des folies dramatiques" where every keyhole into which he peers reveals a paradigm or a metaphor for cinema's illusions: the violation of gravity, reverse motion, a peering eye in countershot, and the composite body of flat graphic elements with human limbs. Cinema itself would thus be a corridor in a hotel of dramatic absurdities, appearing seriatim. At the end of those scenes, he shoots himself in his first suicide.

The Vicomte de Noailles, who paid for *L'age d'or*, also sponsored Cocteau's film. He appeared in the film, with his wife, along with friends of the nobility, in a theatrical loge overlooking the penultimate episode of the suicide of the poète as a card-player, who snatched his inspiration from the corpse of an adolescent killed by a marble snowball. Noailles and his friends demanded Cocteau reshoot the scene without them when they saw he had them applaud a suicide. (Noailles himself did not appear in the comparable scene in *L'Age d'or*, so it remained uncensored.)

The card sharp plays against the Muse who walks off through the snow without leaving footprints. Their absences are as significant a negative symbol of cinematographic inscription as the positive footprints in beach sand Deren showed to conclude her *At Land* (1944).

The Horse's Mouth is a realist comedy. So too, Bratby's expressionistic paintings are tied to the realism to which the 'Kitchen Sink' school adhered. Although Jimson attributed his 'conversion' to art to encountering a Matisse painting that 'skinned his eyes,' his work in the film owes very little to the French master. Although the film-critical press called *Le sang d'un poète* a 'Surrealist' film, it's true affinities were to allegorical Symbolism, as an early title card tell us. Several scenes refer to the Greek Orphic mysteries modernized: such as the Ace of Hearts that the card sharp steals, and the angel who comes from the dead boy's soul.

A self-reflexive title card in Cocteau's film refers to "a documentary of unreal events." He interrupts the fall of a factory tower near the start and completes it near the end to suggest that the entire film has occurred in a split-second. In *The Horse's Mouth*, the wall on which Jimson and his assistants have painted his 'Last Judgment' also tumbled, but only because he himself has driven the wrecking machine to save others the "responsibility" for destroying a "national treasure." Time (and Space) in Neame's films are always realistic.

Neame had worked with Guinness before – most notably on *Tunes of Glory* (1956). In that film as well, his direction was focused on displaying his star's remarkable ability as an actor. Guinness's Jimson is a loveable, grouchy bum, always in need of money, with a love of painting, or rather imagining, murals. The characters of *Le sang d'un poète* are mere models, visible incarnations of ideas without distinguishing traits as people. They were the predecessors of the somnambulistic figures in the films of Maya Deren, Stan Brakhage, Kenneth Anger, Curtis Harrington, and Gregory Markopoulos. At the conclusion of her pamphlet, *An Anagram of Ideas on Art, Form and Film* (1946), Deren called *Le sang d'un poète* "one of the finest films I have seen," praising its "economy of statement.... [whose] meaning depends upon a good many immediately visual images and realities..."

In the end, the symbolic synopsis of the artist's life as inspiration, self-satisfaction, cheating, theft, destruction, ruthlessness, and Orphic apotheosis, as envisioned in *Le sang d'un poète,* is not very different than the fictive biography offered by Cary, Guinness and Neame.

Charlie Chaplin

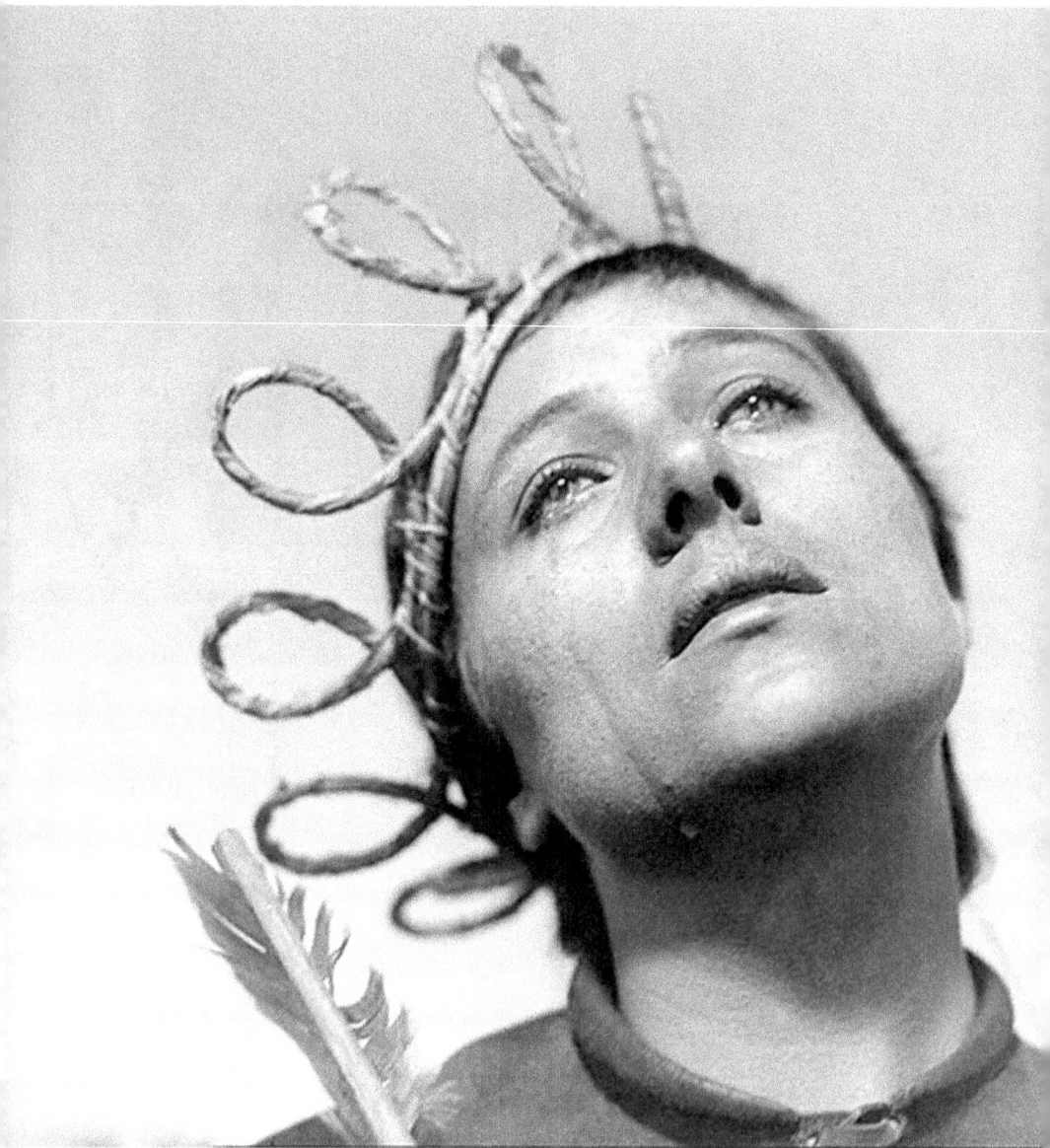

The Passion of Joan of Arc (1928).

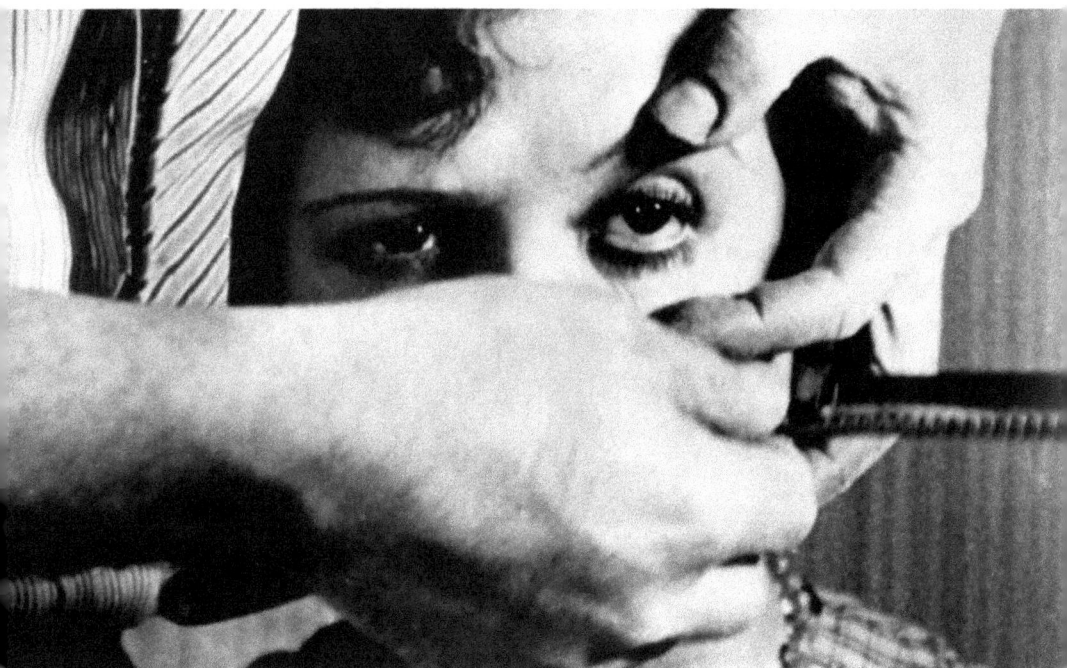

Un Chien Andalou (1929).

Blue Velvet (1986).

The Golden Age (1930).

Vampyr (1932).

Blood of a Poet (1932).

The Horse's Mouth (1958).

Triumph des Willens
[Triumph of the Will]
and
Listen to Britain

In the impressive beginning of *The Triumph of the Will* (1935) an airplane passes through clouds from the point of view of a pilot. We do not see a person until Hitler steps out of the landed plane, saluting. He is the avatar of the Sun, bringing the light from above the clouds to medieval Old Town of Nürenburg in order to bestow order on its ancient streets amid wildly cheering and saluting crowds. Filmmaker Leni Riefenstahl admitted she had thought Hitler "the greatest man who ever lived."

In 'Homecoming' Hölderlin wrote of the Romantic topos that Riefenstahl invoked at the start of her film:

Meanwhile the silver heights gleam peacefully above,
...
And yet higher up still above the light there dwells the pure
Blissful god rejoicing in the play of holy beams
Silent he dwells alone, and brightly shines his countenance,
The heavenly one seems disposed to give life, to create joy, with us, as
often when, conscious of measure,
Conscious of all that breathes, hesitant too and sparing, the god
Sends to cites and houses most gentle happiness...

Humphrey Jennings's *Listen to Britain* (1942) reverses this trope to end with the song of Empire ("Rule Britannia") rising from the clouds of smoke from wartime factories, heralding Allied victory over the world. German airplanes (unseen) merely drop bombs at night; they do not transport saving gods from the Empyrean. Until that final moment *Listen to Britain* plays down its propagandistic dimension, preferring subtle indications of national unity: such as the populist duo of Flanagan and Allen singing to cheerful factory workers while Myra Hess, a German exile from the Nazis, plays Mozart in the National Gallery to an upper-class audience, including the Queen and a wounded soldier. Outside, the statue of Nelson in Trafalgar Square hints that, yet again, the ultimate heroic victory is at hand.

While children play in a northern schoolyard, a framed portrait of a uniformed Scot indicates that a father is at war. Jennings shows the bomb shelters in London but none of the painful effects of German blitz that can be found in his *London Can Take It* (1940) or *The Fires Were Started* (1943). As the title indicate, *Listen to Britain* stresses the sounds of the wartime nation: a female ambulance crew singing "The Ash Grove" in their underground shelter, Canadian volunteers singing "Home on the Range" on a blacked-out train, factory whistles, airplane defenses, the BBC world reports, humming workers, soldiers and civilians dancing at Blackpool to "Roll Out the Barrel," etc. His camera isolates several attractive men and women, of different classes, to counterbalance the hundreds of blonde beauties Riefenstahl showed hysterically welcoming the Fuhrer to Nürenburg and the chorus of fit young men exercising.

There may be a touch of class criticism in the way Jennings and his editor, Stuart McAllister, cut from the enthusiastic reception of Flanagan and Allen to the Queen rudely kibitzing with the art historian, Kenneth Clark, while Hess plays. Clark was then the director of the National Gallery. After moving the paintings to protect them from the Blitz, he made the Gallery available for free daily concerts.

Jennings and McAllister dissolved the sound of Mozart's piano into the noise of an armament factory, then to that of a military band playing "A Life on the Ocean Waves," until the stirring chorus sings "Rule Britannia" as the smoke of the factory rises in the sky.

Humphrey Jennings' brilliant documentary film makes no direct allusion to Len Riefenstahl's great record of the 1934 Nazi rally in Nürenburg. Nevertheless, it reverses its heroic typology.

Bringing Up Baby
and
There's Something About Mary

Stanley Cavell said just about everything worth saying about *Bringing Up Baby* (1938) in his *Pursuits of Happiness* (1984). Now, about forty years later, I shall add some irrelevancies. It may have been easier to be funny when there was a code about what might not be said or represented in a film. When the code prescribed that unmarried partners in a bed may be symbolized only by shoes beside the bed, Leo McCary attained a pinnacle of hilarity in *Duck Soup* (1933) when the libidinous Harpo Marx (as Paul Revere) rode into a woman's bedroom. After a fade out, we see her shoes, Harpo's' shoes, and between them horseshoes beside the bed. Was it a *ménage à trois* or did the horse discreetly separate the couple?

When we think back to the origins of comedy, we come to the Greek theater. That theater was fundamentally and most importantly a religious event. Going to see the plays, producing the plays, writing the plays were elements of a religious festival. Now there is some serious question as to whether or not women were even allowed to attend the performances. Maybe they were, maybe they weren't. Classicists are divided about that. One thing is absolutely known: *no* women performed on stage. *All* the female roles in tragedy were played by men. *All* the female roles in comedy were played by men. Now in comedy this gets a little more complicated because the oldest comedy in Greek was *ithyphallic*. It is called "Old Comedy" to distinguish it from what is called "New Comedy," which we would understand as "Situation Comedy," that is the comic tradition that has really lasted in our theater, film, and television. Initially, one knew it was a comedy performance because all the actors who appeared on stage, whether they were playing men or women, wore a prosthetic penis. They came out with a phallus. Some of them came riding out on a big, long one, others came out swinging one, some had little wrinkled up ones. All through the performance they had their prosthetic penises out. Now it seems that the Greeks thought there was something a little funny about the male member. They seem to be right, if you look at the movies and the tradition. There is something a bit comic about the male investment in that small tube of flesh.

In *Bringing Up Baby*, scene after scene turns on the repressed idea of *coitus a tergo more ferrarum.* probably because the titular 'Baby' is a leopard. Susan (played by Katherine Hepburn) has fallen in love at first sight with a paleontologist, Dr. David Huxley (Cary Grant) who must fit a fossil bone into his dinosaur to complete its reconstructed skeleton. The first indirect mention of *coitus a tergo* occurs so early in the film we could hardly notice it. Huxley speculates to his fiancée assistant, Miss Swallow, that "perhaps [the fossil bone] goes in the tail;" to which she replies, "Nonsense! You tried that last night…" She is called Miss Swallow as if she were a small ornithological specimen or an accomplished fellatrix. Susan calls Huxley 'Mr. Bone,' referring to both his paleontological obsession and his potential erection.

When the fierce little dog, George, seizes and buries the fossil, they search for it on her wealthy aunt's Connecticut property. (Baby belongs to the aunt.) In the most magical moment of the film, they come upon Baby and George playing roughhouse at night. For Susan, "they like each other" but David frets that "in a moment my bone will be lost forever." (In *There's*

Something About Mary (1998) the much-abused dog Mary shares with Magda, attacked Ben's crotch.) Just before the scene of the two animals cavorting, Susan had crouched on all fours in her search for the missing bone. David, failing as usual to understand her, scolded, "Susan, this is no time to play squat-tag." Trying to reach Baby and George, they both fall into a stream. Susan tells David, "We are right back where we started, only now I am wet." The writers of *Bringing Up Baby* loaded the film with such double-entendres as if deliberately trying to defy or circumvent the Code of forbidden topics. At one point, after Susan has hidden and laundered David's clothes to keep him near her, her aunt asks him why he is wearing a frilly woman's night coat. He shouts back at her, "I've gone gay!" as if to confirm the persistent rumors of Grant's bisexuality. Ultimately, Miss Swallow departs, and Susan wins David Huxley.

One of her early attempts to draw his attention takes place in a fancy restaurant where they are both formally attired. Stepping on the edge of her gown, he accidentally ripped the back off of it, and hastily claps his tophat over her buttocks. She demands, "Will you please stop doing that with your hat?" until she realizes that her underwear is exposed, then she makes him exit, walking close behind her, as if in *coitus a tergo*. The very subversion of the code of decency contributes to the hilarity of the film.

Ever since *Fast Times in Ridgemont High* (1982) there have been masturbation scenes in Hollywood movies. When men do it, it's almost always funny. When women do it, it's another matter. I'm not referring just to pornography. The religious Greek theater saw something really important about the exposure of erotic desire and the oddity in the male index of erotic desire. I was very delighted to learn that Peter Farrelly, who directed *There's Something About Mary* with his brother, Bobby Farrelly had a rather unique way of dealing with people who work in his films – that is, producers, actors, and crew. He is known for exposing himself to each person that he is considering hiring. One person described his rather unique ways of doing it. When he was talking about having a melanoma and he was going to show that it was on his waist and he said, "you gotta lean forward and look." And he lifted his shirt to reveal the head of his penis sticking up just above his underpants. When they were casting Cameron Diaz for the film, one of the ways in which he wanted to see if she was the right actress for the film was, of course, how she responded to him when he exposed himself in this way to her. And she burst out laughing, calling him a "creative genius." He said, "You're perfect! You're going to be my *narrator* in the film." Marx Brothers themselves were notorious for their naughty exposure of themselves at various occasions.

One of the things that is great about *There's Something About Mary* is its phallic humor. We should keep in mind *all* the great comic figures had a certain kind of phallic style, even before it was possible to expose the *membrum virile* in film. I am thinking of Chaplin's cane and his hat, or the use of the hats generally. Keaton, whose onscreen character was sexually so naive, wears this little, tiny hat. The gags that Harpo Marx would play with his hat fall into this category. In *Duck Soup* there's this wonderful *ithyphallic* dimension in that he is constantly reaching for his horns, his virtual testicles, and cutting off the feathers or any other phallic protuberance of any rival male, such as cutting their hats. Think of Woody Allen who describes himself in one of his films as the only man who has penis envy.

If we go back to 1982, to *Fast Times at Ridgemont High* in which the actor, Judge Reinhold, is caught jerking off in the bathroom by Phoebe Cates, we have an introduction of the humor of explicit phallic desire in American comedy. In the Farrellys' film. our protagonist, Mary, is an extremely interesting character because they do not deny her sexuality. Howard Hawks merely implies it in *Bringing Up Baby*. Mary is very explicit about what she is interested in. She is truly a figure of an open heart, looking for a thoroughly good man. For all other matters, as she says, she has her vibrator, which will take care of that. She has a very interesting and subtle character development.

But the greatest aspect of this film is the camera; I mean the film's cinematic intelligence. Now I saw this film by sheer accident, I was summering in Rhode Island, and I went to the movies one Saturday night and the theater was packed – it was the opening night of the film. And from the titles on, the audience was on the floor. I wasn't on the floor from the titles – it took me two or three minutes before I was down among the spilled popcorn. But the reason the audience was in hysterics was it was a Rhode Island audience, and the film starts at a Rhode Island high school that they all knew. It was probably the last time that I have been to a commercial movie in which I lost more than two-thirds of the dialogue and the scenes because I was rolling in the muck on the bottom of the theater screaming out for help to save my life. But there was no chance of getting any kind of emergency assistance because several hundred other people were dying of laughter at the same time. I had to go back the next night to see what I had missed. What amazed me was the wonderful cinematographic intelligence – the use of camera placement, the use of the camera – understanding that these are really very, very good filmmakers.

The motto of this film, which I take to be the motto of all great comedy, is: *I'm just fucking with you*. Both in the metaphorical sense that comedy fucks with us and in the religious, ancient Greek sense, a good comedy fucks us as well. We can see wonderfully in the final titles of this film the degree to which the Farrellys were committed to fucking with us all throughout the film. During every scene that they shot that ended up in the film and many of the outtakes, they did a musical number, which culminates in the final choral movement that recognizes that this film is a series of choruses They also employ choruses of words: e.g. Warren's repetition of *frank and beans* at various moments, emphasizing the intuitive underlining (rather than academically underlining) the relationship of this film to the very origins of comedy (as I am doing now.)

When I first saw the film, I had a sense of its cinematic genius from an early moment: the close-up of Ben Stiller's mouth after Mary invites him to be her prom date; the camera moves in not too dramatically, but just enough on his braces. Had it not been for the tutelage of Adolfas Mekas when I was very young and watching him work and talking to him about making comedy, I probably never would have noticed this touch. But in many of the great scenes of this film, the comic handling of the camera is quite brilliant.

The first scene I want to discuss is painful to almost every one of the male persuasion watching this film. As soon as Mary's stepfather (a brilliant piece of casting – the original script did not call for an African-American, but this was just a wonderful piece of casting and the first instance of 'I'm just fucking with you,' as he says). Peter and Bobby Farrelly have a younger sister. Apparently, whenever a date came for her, their father fucked with the date by giving him a really hard time. When the little girl was having a party celebrating her 12th birthday, one of the boys invited to the party went into the bathroom and didn't come out for a long time. The parents had to go in to help him because of the extraordinarily painful thing that happened with his zipper. Not quite the level of *frank and beans* that we see in this scene, but what is wonderful about the reconstruction of that disaster in the film is the understanding that the most fundamental piece of narrative, cinematic rhetoric, is the countershot. You can't have a traditional feature film without having a shot of someone looking and then what the person sees, or someone speaking and the person they are speaking to, back and forth across an axis of 180 degrees. We expect it all the time. Without it, a film looks stagey; it looks flat.

Now of course the greatest films ever made, such as *Ordet* (1955) of Dreyer, or *Persona* of Bergman, or *The Puppetmaster* (1993) of Hou Hsiao Hsien find ways of avoiding or sparing shot-counter-shot. But basically, in the bathroom scene we expect there to be a countershot of what these several observers are seeing, but of course we know because it is his penis and his testicles, we shall never see a countershot. However, they milk this scene over and over again, quite brilliantly with character after character after character coming in, and each one of them having a different reaction to what they're seeing, and of course we know we're never going to get 'the money shot' – to use the term from pornography, a term used in this film by Healy, when he uses his binoculars to ogle the breasts of Mary and instead gets those of Magda, (which are prosthetic to stress ugilness.). So, this delay in Ben's bathroom scene serves to construct the money shot as a comic device...

Then we see a great dolly-shot of the whole family listening. I hope you noticed what Warren was doing when they enter. He was working on a Rubix Cube, which he solved during the scene. The camera will pan slightly, following him and then give us a detail shot, and back with a countershot. He has to put glasses on to emphasize the visual dimension of the sequence. That should be enough, but the Farallys know the fun of it. They top it with this hilarious line, that the mother can help because she's *a dental hygienist*. Then they repeat the whole sequence without showing the money shot, with her reaction... and then a reaction to the sound of her reaction. Here *frank and beans is* introduced. Warren picks up on it immediately. Already the scene is so prolonged that we are convinced we're never going to see 'the money shot.' Before Stiller can explain how he managed the double trouble, the cop has to come in. Then in comes the fireman. *He* will see the money shot that we never expected to. They all see it before we do. The fireman has to call outside to attract more people. In fact, it was so important that the Farrellys had constructed for it a three-foot high pair of pants with a zipper and with a bubble apparatus. Part of the brilliance is that, although we do see *it* in the end, we see *nothing*, because the visual recognition of the penis requires to see the *glans penis* and the testicles (or at least the testicles without the *glans penis*, or the *glans penis* without the testicles). Here we just see a little glob, but it is so funny and so wonderfully timed and so brilliantly constructed that it is one of the great pieces of modern cinema. This is hilariously fused with the sentimental image of the birds on the windowsill.

Of course, the construction of the house is completely illogical, because you wouldn't have a sight line to the girl's dressing room from the bathroom window. We hear stupid sentimental singing, which then leads to rack-focusing. The whole event is a preliminary suggestion of the masturbation scene that is to come so much later. After the singing birds, we hear the sound of a zipper louder than normally possible. The spectacular auditory effect is emphasized by the outdoor scene of the mother rushing the adolescent away. Rather than showing the blood, the comic effect is created by the sound of the unzipping and the elliptical cut to "we have a bleeder," with Warren repeating, "*Frank and beans*...."

The film is very carefully constructed for its moral lesson. It's very important that Ted intervenes on behalf of Warren before anyone knows that Warren is Mary's brother. He is supposed to stay in his yard, but he has come to school, presumably for the first time. So, Ted is not doing anything to win Mary's favor when he steps in. Ted's good nature appears when he calls the football hero to clarify the situation, so that Mary can get help from the nearly perfect man, in Ted's view.

This film operates on a rather wonderful fiction that is somewhat contrary to the common cliché – that gorgeous women prefer men who make them laugh, to great hunks. The film argues that what she really wants is 'a good sport.' And all through the film Ted is a good sport. This is a very important principle for Peter Farrelly in particular. Ben Stiller didn't want to do the masturbation scene. And Diaz was skeptical about doing the hair scene. But they had to be good sports for the film. In a move so typical of what Adolfas Mekas would do, we have a scene of presumably gay men having sex at the rest stop. They are really the crew of the film – all the electricians, the camera men, the assistants, etc. They all agreed to be lying there in their underwear. This homage to the crew is worthy of Adolfas Mekas. One of the guys in jail is, I believe, Diaz's father. Ben Stiller's family is also in the film. Everybody in a Farrelly film has to be a good sport. For them, the highest moral quality is to be a good sport.

The famous masturbation scene is prolonged in interesting ways. We see Ted first in the bathroom. Then we cut outside to Woogie noticing Mary, the set is very carefully designed with two prominent colors. On the one hand, a blue curtain in a blueish room represents the bathroom, while the rest is in a bright pink. And it's important that the door be open to firmly the establish the communicating space between these two rooms. Notice how very carefully the filmmakers position the camera, so that we only see the right side of Stiller's face, especially after his orgasm. But it wouldn't be sufficiently comic just to keep the camera on the right side of his face. He must move his head in various ways. Even when the there is a cut from a medium shot to a long shot, it is along the same axis (where we would normally expect a slight shift of axis). It is done to hide his ear. If not consciously, at least unconsciously, we can be reassured that we have seen his entire body. We don't have a clue that there is semen dripping from his ear. And of course there's this wonderful cut after she takes it and puts it on her hair; I mean the cut to the restaurant, where the waitress's long hair calls attention to the issue of hair; we get back to Ted talking to her, and then only then, when she's talking about the idea of Healy being a murderer (Ted needs to find out whether she actually had sexual intercourse with him) our entire attention is riveted on the wave of her hair held fixed by ejaculate.

The masturbation scene begins with the music of Bizet. The camera will pan up from the black-and-white newspaper and then cut away, shifting tone as well with the music, to Woogie standing outside, realizing that Mary is there. Then it goes back to the camera on the right side of Ted's face. By now we're so completely used to the right side of the face we don't expect to see the left side. Meanwhile, Woogie is reacting to seeing Mary unexpectedly. At the climax of Bizet there is a cut to the crumpling the newspaper the moment Ben orgasms, and then in a close-up his eyes roll back. Notice how they cut to the same axis rather than shifting angle, so we still don't see the left ear. His head almost turns towards us until we have a sense, we're seeing the whole face. He looks up. He looks down. He turns his head quickly. The speed with which he turns around here keeps us from seeing his earlobe. By carefully keeping his ear off to the side in this shot, and we hardly notice that he is being framed from the right all the time. Finally, we see where the semen went! The Farrallys tried the episode once with the question, "is that cum?" but it didn't work. We only see the edge of Mary's face, several times from several angles. All the time he's interrogating her about sexual intercourse, we are watching her with a semen-frozen hair.

There is a continual tendency in the film to pull away from any concept of realism, in a kind of Brechtian gesture, of incorporating the music. Very often we hear music of bands in the background of films, but in this film the musicians are in the most incongruous place... always showing the guitarist and the drummer barely moving at all. At the very end of the film when Ben is crying on the street, the drummer was crying as well. The film thrives on little touches like that, as when in the scene in the apartment, when Magda comes out with the old man behind her, you notice what she was eating – a banana split.

Near the end of the film, Ben turns off the TV. We hear music and we assume it's just background music, because he's alone. When the camera tracks towards him, he takes an overly sentimental picture: we get the insert shot, then another angle on the shot. The camera, peering in the window will track back from the TV set, until we see snow, shot in Miami (it's supposed to be Providence). There's our chorus on the street of Providence in middle of winter. The choral dimension of *There's Something About Mary* is an unintentional homage to his Aristophanic sources. The success of the film owes much to the Farallys' ability to fuse the 'gross out' genre with the 'chick flick.'

Vredens Dag [Day of Wrath]
and
Sommardsnattens leende
[Smiles of a Summer's Night]

When Jay Leyda wrote *Films beget Films* (1964), he was the first to apply to cinema what we all knew about the other arts: poems beget poems, symphonies engender symphonies, one great painting calls forth another. Without fully realizing it, the greatest of film historians set the agenda for subsequent criticism and analysis. His program was so positive, that later critics, such as I, were free to develop the negative route.

Sometimes a filmmaker will deliberately invoke a rival's great film to diminish its glory. When Ingmar Bergman took Carl Theodor Dreyer's *Vredens Dag* [*Day of Wrath*] (1943) as the model for his *Sommarnattens leende* [*Smiles of a Summer Night*] (1955), he was much less benign than Tarkovsky was to be toward Bergman himself when he constructed *Zerkalo*. Bergman viciously parodied Dreyer's tragedy and turned it into his own most successful comedy. *Vredens Dag* may be the most morally complex film ever made, but Bergman ignored its subtleties, if he perceived them. (Few of Dreyer's critics have.) Because the film was made in Nazi-occupied Denmark in 1943, and because it concerns witchcraft, many have refused the filmmaker's denial and insisted that it is an allegory of Nazi oppression. The evidence of the film itself clearly belies such an interpretation. The argument for that position entailed the following false steps: (1) all "reasonable people" knew in 1943 that witchcraft never had existed; (2) Anne's confession to being a murderous witch at the end of the film was merely an act of resignation in the face of a woman's hopeless situation and betrayed love. Of course, the assumption of having all "reasonable people" on one's side (and the denial of evidence) are the hallmarks of tyranny, as practiced by every political partisan.

Dreyer deliberately cast the film to foster such errors. Anne and Martin are played sympathetically by attractive matinée idols. Habitual film viewers "know" and look forward to the confirmation that they are destined to love one another. Conversely, Martin's grandmother, Merete, is a prune-faced old hag who is mean and disrespectful to Anne (even though she is usually right all through the film). Myriad films assure us of her eventual comeuppance. Her son, Absalom, is played by a slow-moving aged man – an icon of impotence – even though Dreyer had to fight off the producers who wanted a more vigorous older man in the role (a "Renaissance type" as prescribed by Wiers-Jennsen's play which the film adapts). Yet Dreyer was at pains to signal to his viewers that Martin alone could sexually and emotionally satisfy Anne. He baited a trap for those who judge by casting.

On the other hand, the filmmaker made several changes in the text of *Anne Petersdotter* (Hans Wiers-Jenssen's play) to underline the actuality of witchcraft and the guilt of Anne. The opening scene, a long complex, sinuous shot, was his innovation; in it the witch Herlofs Marte profits from selling "evil" herbs and escapes through a pigpen from a crowd of denouncers. In the play she does not know whether or not she is a witch; in the film, there is no doubt (except for those viewers who transcendentally know better, certain that witchcraft never existed). When she is being tortured, she effectively cursed Laurentius who died soon after, in another of Dreyer's innovations.

From their first meeting Dreyer's Anne has an uncanny feeling of having known Martin. Wiers-Jenssen makes no mystery of this, explicitly pointing out that Anne, who is a few years Martin's senior, once hid the boy to protect him from a drunk he had teased. In the play, Martin doubts the nature of witchcraft, but Dreyer's film denied him that doubt, just as he eliminated all the conversations between father and son portraying the old priest as an exhausted liberal reformer. Dreyer reenforced the play's caricature of Merete as an overbearing mother-in-law, cutting all the passages humanizing her. If she had known that her son had spared Anne's mother from burning as a witch out of lust for her young daughter (as Herlofs Marte revealed to Anne), (apparently, she does not), her behavior would be justified as a fusion of disgust and protection toward her son. Those who want the film to be an allegory of Nazi oppression would have a better case, anachronistically, for the stage play, *Anne Petersdotter* (1908). We are even encouraged to applaud silently when Anne, now in love with Martin, defies her mother-in-law by citing an erotic passage from the Song of Songs which Dreyer added to the drama.

In three magnificent outdoor scenes, Dreyer invented a mini-exposé of Anne's obsessive passion for Martin and his growing anxiety about their unnatural, "incestuous" affair. As I wrote in "Landscape in the Cinema: The Rhythms of the World and the Camera," and reworked in *Brakhage, Straub/ Huillet. Deleuze and the Philosophy of Modern Cinema*:

> Dreyer located the rare excursions out of the interiors, where most of his tragedy of Sixteenth Century repression and adultery occurs [and all of Wiers-Jenssen's drama], in a setting where symbolic hints of the fallenness of nature disturb their illicit idylls. Each time the lovers, a young woman and the son of her aged husband, go out of their home the landscape reflects in varying degrees their amorous illusions and their bitter consequences: Their first and most innocent excursion ends when they see someone gathering wood to burn the witch [Herlofs Marte]. At the turning point of the film, after they have fallen in love, the woman reads the image of a tree and its reflection in water as an

image of the fusion of ideal lovers, but the young man sees it as barren narcissism. Despite the wind storm that accompanies the woman's acknowledgment of the demonic quality of her hatred for her elderly husband, and the dense fog that engulfs them when the son breaks off their relationship after his father's death, Dreyer invests the film with such a thorough moral ambiguity that the unquestionably symbolic landscape sustains two incompatible interpretations, in which the sources of the tragedy lies alternately in the reckless will of the young protagonists or in the repressive society of the elder representatives of religious order.

Instead of these three instances of morally sublime weather, the lusty servant, Firth, of *Sommarnattens leende* proclaims the three erotic smiles of the Swedish summer night.

Whereas Dreyer's opening two shots compare and contrast the aged women, Herlofs Marte and Merete (played by two actresses, then in their Seventies who had played hundreds of roles in the Danish theatre), Bergman invented a naughty old dowager in a baroque castle to preside over the magical resorting of lovers to their appropriate partners, as the mother of Désirée Armfeldt.

Both Dreyer's Martin and Bergman's Henrik are studying to be clergymen. The former aspires to his father's theological learning and authority, but Henrik's father, a womanizing lawyer married to a child-bride (who secretly loves Henrik) mercilessly derides his son's vocation. In a particularly vicious bit of comedy, he comes home early from a play starring his former mistress, Désirée Armfeldt, to find his son sexually compromised with his wife's maid. He mocks the young man's phallic guitar and drinks his champagne (the symbol of his premature ejaculation) while advising him to remount immediately after falling from a horse. In acting this way, the father ignored the warning Désirée uttered in the fragment of the play he had just seen against never humiliating a man's pride. He will later pay the price for it, when his wife runs off with his son, leaving him to collect the symbolical veil of the virginity she had preserved all through their marriage.

Bergman is on record for complaining that Ulla Jacobsson,

who played the child-bride, Anne Egerman, was visibly pregnant during her elopement with Henrik. Nevertheless, her pregnancy proleptically fulfills the fantasy she expressed during her marriage to Frederick Egerman and more pointedly, it overturns one of the key visual markers of Dreyer's direction in *Vredens Dag*: just prior to the image of the reflected tree that Martin understands as an emblem of narcissism, Anne took him by the hand away from Absalom, whose eye falls on a stencil frame for her embroidery of a naked young mother holding her toddler by the hand. In case the viewers have forgotten that Anne has substituted her stepson for the baby she will not get from Absalom, the filmmaker forces the point upon them. Bergman, in turn, briefly put a piece of embroidery in the hands of the child-bride, whom he also named Anne.

From the start, the lawyer, Frederick Egerman, has all the attributes of a phallic man: his pen, his cigar, and a walking stick. He struts past a series of large ornamental cannon to visit his new wife. When humiliating his son, he tells him all young love is narcissism ("self-love and love of love"). During his clandestine visit to Désirée backstage at the theatre, he meets his current rival, her lover, Count Malcolm, a distorted mirror image of his pride and lust, whose phallic paraphernalia includes a horse and a noisy antique car. Ultimately, Malcolm challenges Frederik to a duel of Russian roulette. For several minutes, the viewers think that Frederick, like Dreyer's Absalom, is dead – the sacrificial victim of the drama, until Malcolm laughingly admits he filled the pistol with soot. In the elaborate transformation of lovers, Bergman apparently drew on Shakespeare's *A Midsummer Night's Dream* to supplement *Dies Irae*. (The filmmaker had staged Shakespeare's play twice in the early Forties, before *Vredens Dag* was made.)

Dreyer pioneered the long shot, moving camera, style of his later films in *Vredens Dag*, especially when he departed from *Anne Petersdotter*. Bergman's debt to his long experience as a director of plays can be seen in the frequent substitution of shot-countershot with shots of two characters in dialogue, side by side, facing the camera. Yet Bergman's greatest achievement in *Sommarnattens leende* was to change Dreyer's moral tragedy of violating the incest taboo into a completely satisfying comic farce. Comedy has the power of reducing the sort of moral dilemma that fascinated Dreyer into an irrelevant triviality.

Lysis
and
Vertigo

After I thought that I had completed this book of Incongruous Pairings, I presented a introduction to Gregory Markopoulos' trilogy, *Du Sang, de la Voluptè, et de la Mort* (1947-48) at Light Industry in Brooklyn, New York. I may have infected myself with the "pairing" virus but seeing *Lysis* (1948) for the first time in decades elicited from me a comparison to Hitchcock's *Vertigo* (1958), on which I wrote in *The Hidden God* (2003) and revised in *Marvelous Names* (2023). The comparison in this case turns on my dubious identification and interpretation of the myth of Persephone in both films.

In my earlier readings of *Vertigo*. I had speculated that the color scheme of the film, its Orphic mystery, the use of vegetation, and above all the story of "mad Carlotta" suggested elements from the "Homeric Hymn to Demeter," where Carlotta was a false figuration of Demeter, and the two Bay Area seasons mistakenly reflected the absence and the return of Persephone from the realm of the Dead. I identified the woman in a white gown early in *Lysis* as a figure for Persephone. Markopoulos found myth to be the truth of life, while Hitchcock implied it is a pagan fraud, distracting us from the truth of Roman Catholic religion (as movies do, in Hitchcock's self-critical imagination).

Lysis takes its title from Plato's early dialogue on *philia* (passionate friendship), but the dialogue does little to account for the imagery of the film. It is rather an autobiography in images of the young filmmaker, who appears in it himself after a montage of photographs, paintings, and objects from his childhood. We see him wandering around industrial Toledo, Ohio beside the Maumee River when a series of mythological scenes interrupt or attract his reveries. The film indicates that they are essential parts of his consciousness.

The first of these shows a tall woman in a white gown emerging from, and later descending into, an underground staging space in what seems to be Toledo's neohellenic Ottawa amphitheater. She is barefoot and often walks on tiptoe. I assume Markopoulos noted Persephone's initial epithet in the "Homeric Hymn to Demeter": *tanuphoron* (thin-ankled) and subsequently identified her by shooting a closeup of her bare feet. Additionally, like Persephone in the Homeric Hymn, she picks flowers and gazes at her reflection in a pool.

Insofar as *Lysis* is a meditation of the self, the mythological scenes constitute confessions of the filmmaker's obsessive recognition of Greek myth everywhere he points his camera. The culmination of this vision of the world illuminated by ancient myths would be *The Iliac Passion* (1967), although that notion is evident throughout Markopoulos's long artistic career. Thomas Beard pointed out to me that the French title for the trilogy comes from Maurice Barrès's travel memoir of the same title. Quite appropriately, before publishing *Du sang, de la volupté, de la mort* in 1893, Barrès wrote his *trilogie de moi*, a Symbolist account of the cult of the self. For Hitchcock, as I argued in *The Hidden God* and *Marvelous Names*, the mythos and the fantasy of reincarnation in *Vertigo* were merely foils to lure viewers away from foreseeing the underlying murder mystery.

In 1955 Markopoulos showed the film trilogy at the French Institute in Athens where he introduced the three films with the text "Psyche's Search of the Herb of Invulnerability." There he demonstrated how distant the three films were from their nominal sources in Pierre Louÿs and Plato. He did not indicate his mythographic sources, but they were much more abstruse than the familiar Cupid and Psyche story in Apuleius's *Metamorphoses*, The "herb of invulnerability" seems to have come from the *Biblioteca* of pseudo-Apollodorus while allusions to the cult of Eros in Boetia might have been the result of his reading of Pausanias.

Markopoulos was a marvel of unwavering self-confidence as a filmmaker. He reveled in the liberties he gave himself with his sources. In *Lysis*, for example, he cast an African-American woman as Leda, and his Prometheus resembles iconic pictures of Saint Sebastian. He equally cherished the way his films changed in structure and theme while he was shooting and editing them.

Color and costume are as important to all of Markopoulos's films as they would have been for *Vertigo*. He stated so explicitly in "Psyche's Search for the Herb of Invulnerability," when he declared: "Color reflects the true character of the individual before us, whether it be on the screen, in a painting, or in the street". Persephone's white dress rhymes with the lace-embroidered baptismal pillow seen in several shots from the first part of the *Lysis*, as if she emerged from his native heritage.

Triumph of the Will (1935).

Listen To Britain (1942).

Bringing Up Baby (1938).

There's Something About Mary (1998).

Day of Wrath (1943).

Smiles of a Summer Night (1955).

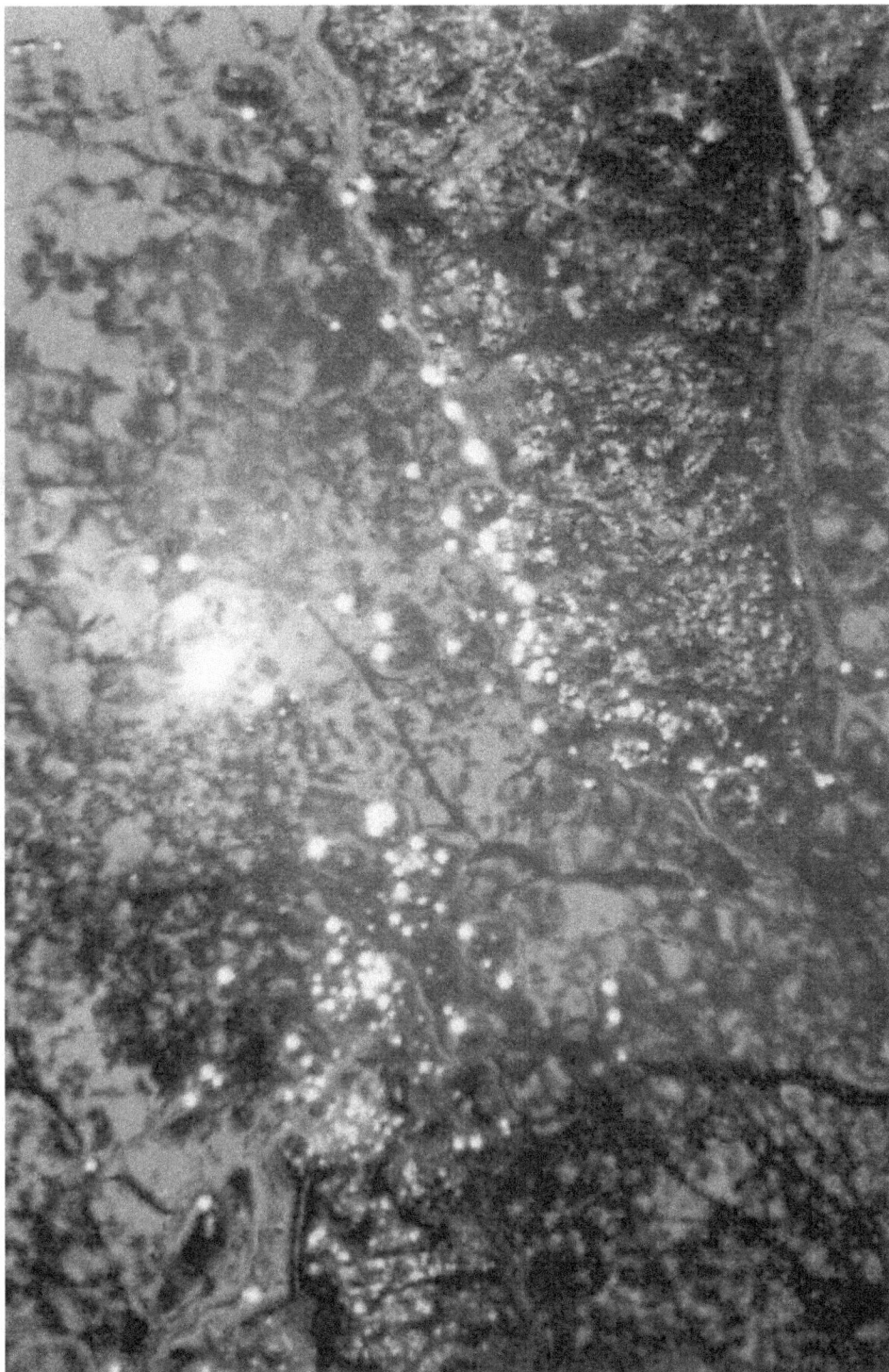

Lysis (1948).

Vertigo (1957).

Rashomon
and
Les vacances de M. Hulot
[*Mr. Hulot's Holiday*]

In this chapter I seem to be following the principle of Ken Kelman's lectures, which I edited, in putting together two more or less contemporary films to illustrate an historical turning point. I lectured on this 'double bill' nearly every year in the film history course I offered at Princeton University,

In Kelman's brilliant essay, "Classic Plastics and Total Tectonics," the former category refers to the plastic organization of the silent films, *Zemlya* [*Earth*}] (1930) and *Sunrise* (1927), while "Total Tectonics" refers to the overall architecture of Stan Brakhage's *Anticipation of the Night, The Dead* (1959) and anticipates Markopoulos' *Twice A Man* (1963), as films that eschew breaking down into scenes

Although Kelman acknowledged the role Maya Deren's films plays in the evolution of Total Tectonics, he overlooked two films of 1950 and 1953 that were harbingers of its emergence: I refer to Akira Kurosawa's *Rashomon* (1950; U.S.: 1951) and Jacques Tati's *Les vacances de M. Hulot* [*Mr. Hulot's Holiday*, 1953].

The former had no genetic link to Deren and Alexander Hammid's *Meshes of the Afternoon* (1943) and the latter was just as innocent of the precedent in her *At Land* (1944). *Meshes of the Afternoon* has only two actors who appear in five variants of the same dream. In *Rashomon* three characters tell their versions of a violent rape and murder; One, a woodsman, tells it twice. He also appears in the frame story with two other characters, a priest and a thief.

The torrential rain of the frame story may allegorize the atomic devastation of Japan, and its humiliation. In his astute essay, "*Rashomon* as Modern Art" Parker Tyler compared the film to the panels of Pablo Picasso's "Guernica" and to his "Woman at a Mirror." Each variant of the story has its unique cinematic mode of exposition. At first the camera follows the woodsman through the forest, regularly alternating shots of his face head-on, his walk from the side, and the sun through the trees above him. A series of false point-of view shots mark his discovery of a rope, a woman's sunhat, the cap of her samurai husband, a knife, and an amulet, followed by an "actual" point of view shot from the perspective of a corpse. In sudden fright, he runs off in a series of telephoto swish pans.

The style of first narration emphasizes a single first-person account in order to make the later intersubjective stories more emphatic. We see one man and a series of things that catch his attention: the woman's hat is framed close to camera; it takes a moment to realize this is not a point-of-view shot but that the woodcutter is framed in the background. The same effect is repeated when he looks down at the man's hat, later at the rope, but in both shots the camera is still in front and pans up to him. This makes the tatami shot from the perspective of the dead body of the samurai all the more striking.

In contrast, the priest's narration stresses the luminous couple and the sleeping bandit. If the first story was monomorphic, describing only the evidence found by the lone woodsman, most of the second drama is dyadic: isolating the bandit and the samurai, the bandit and the samurai's wife, then bandit and husband again. During the rape, the sun becomes a sign of wife's sexuality. Tilting camera movements indicate her subjectivity; soft focus her loss of resistance; the knife that falls to the ground where it sticks, the thief's penetration of her.

When the woodcutter, responding to another thief's prodding at the Gate, retells the event as a largely triadic schema, he utterly downplayed all signs of self: he described the crying wife as the bandit proposes marriage to her while the samurai shames and insults her. In a powerful mixture of tatami shots, and mobile closeups, the wife's tears turned to hysterical laughter (usually the sign of the bandit) as she took command of the montage, inducing a swordfight between the two men. What follows is a clownish mess: the antagonists tripped over each other until the bandit finally dispatched the samurai. Her mad reaction began with the camera close to her, then a confined dyad became a complex triad with play between isolated shots of each of three, along with complex triangular compositions. The death of her husband recalled her offscreen presence with scream. The scene ended with longshot and the sound of a birdcall.

Although the third man at the Gate (the second thief) ripped away its wood for firewood at home, further underlying the degradation of traditional Japan after the symbolic rainstorm, the film ended on an optimistic note: the woodcutter adopted a foundling left at the gate, restoring the priest's faith in humanity.

Rashomon was a low budget film, shot completely, outdoors, with only eight actors. The one expensive item was constructing the Rashomon Gate for the frame story. The film is a tour-de-force: same story repeats over and over; there are no interrogators, no resolution; the filmmaker makes much of the shifting symbols (rain, gate, sun, knife, sword). The repetitions with variants unify the film, pushing it in the direction of what Kelman called "total techtonics." Three years later, Jacques Tati unified *Les vacances de M. Hulot* with a complex system of running gags, pushing the feature film even closer to a seamless flow.

According to David Kehr:

Les vacances de M. Hulot is one of the most radical films ever made –
the "Sacre du printemps" of the movies. Without *Les vacances* there
would be no Jean-Luc Godard, no Jean-Marie Straub, no Marguerite
Duras – no modern cinema. With his 1953 film, Jacques Tati drove the
first decisive wedge between cinema and classical narration.

He added that Tati had to find a "non-narrative way of
seeing." There are almost no closeups in the film. The "closeups"
are on the soundtrack. The running gags include: bongs of
restaurant door, the failures and sputtering of Hulot's car, Hulot's
head popping out of attic window of the beach hotel, his efforts to
shake hands culminating in the mistake of him posing as a family
member at a funeral he attended by accident, the henpecked
hotel guest, Henry, following his wife, a business man regularly
taking telephone calls, Hulot's spiraling movements that climax in
his effort to find the end of a hose feeding a spinning sprinkler, to
extinguish a fireworks display he unintentionally set off, etc.
Everywhere he goes, he creates chaos.

Tati's instinct for cinematic invention manifested several
perspectival gags: a photographer looks like a Peeping Tom, an
old tar thinks Hulot's collapsed kayak is a shark, the protagonist's
spiral footprints lead to a wrong man, a man leading a horse
seems to have the horse's head; and even the play of foreground
and background in a single shot produces gags, as when the hotel
waiter cutting a roast, slices a much thicker piece when he sees a
fat man enter the dining room.

The hilarious scene of Hulot adjusting the paintings his
horsewhip knocked to a tilt is even funnier when we realize that
he is not alone in the room. An old man who might have
observed his zany antics is asleep in a chair. That episode
occurred as he waits for his 'date' to go horseback-riding. The
symbolic use of the decorations of the room suggests his sexual
anxiety: a fox throw-rug bites his spur (as a vagina dentata) and
he tries to prop up a candle his whip broke as if it were a flagging
erection.

Tati's film unknowingly follows a pattern set by Maya

Deren's *At Land*. In making *Mashes of the Afternoon* she hit upon a trope that became the basis for her next film: without breaking the rhythm of walking, a figures steps on weeds, sand, and pavement in one continuous, but irrational movement. All of *At Land* expands upon that principle, as the Venus figure (played by Deren herself) emerges from the backward-flowing sea, crawls unnoticed along a crowded dinner table, snatches a chess piece, accompanies a series of four men and finds another in an abandoned shed, and while caressing the hair of two women playing chess, she steals a pawn and runs with it along a beach in a retrograde recapitulation of the events of the film.

Cutting on the unity of bodily movement across disparate spaces performs the same unification that running gags do for *Les vacances*. Tati's means are an intricate series of interlocked repetitions along with a visual style that keeps a distance, refusing to signal gags. The consistency of the Puckish Hulot and the variations on his comic encounters brings the film even closer to Total Tectonics and *Rashomon* had been.

Rear Window
and
Blue Velvet (again)

It is probable that *Blue Velvet* (1986) may owe more to *Rear Window* (1954) than any other pair of films in this book, even than *Zerkelo* to *Persona*. David Lynch was so secretive (or duplicitous) about his influences and borrowings that we have no concrete evidence that he even saw Hitchcock's film.

Rear Window explores the psychology of voyeurism. L.B. Jeffries, an internationally known photographer, is laid up in his New York apartment with his leg in a cast. He spends his time watching his neighbors: when the dancer, 'Miss Torso", does her practice gyrations, he uses a backscratcher to reach into his cast to soothe his itch, in a scene clearly evoking masturbation.

Thus, almost from the start of the film Hitchcock inflects his voyeurism sexually. He also framed the film as an allegory of filmmaking and film viewing. The vulgar metaphors of Jeffrey's visiting nurse-therapist, Stella, abets the latent equation of the sexual undercurrent. (At one point, she tells him that formerly Peeping Toms had their eyes burned out "with a red-hot poker.") The injured photographer is both a filmmaker and a viewer. He uses his binoculars to get closeup views and eventually he employs the telephoto lens of his reflex still camera to get even closer. His wheelchair is a limited dolly. Lisa Freemont, Jefferey's high society girlfriend, combines the two motives of sexuality and filmmaking by calling her overnight lingerie, a "preview of coming attractions." For the most part, the editing of *Rear Window* exemplifies what Hitchcock called "pure" cinema. By that he meant a version of the Kuleshov effect. Lev Kuleshov filmed an expressionless shot of a famous actor, which he intercut with a bowl of soup, a dead young woman in a coffin, and a laughing baby. Viewers praised the subtlety of the actor's skill in portraying hunger, grievous pity, and grandfatherly joy. Hitchcock included facial reactions of his principal actor, and in one retelling of the Kuleshov experiment, characteristically substituted a gourmet meal, a scantily dressed women, and a dead baby for the objects of his sight. Stewart's smile at Miss Torso and at the middle-aged sculptor generates the opposite effects of lust and disdain.

Hitchcock's earlier film, *Spellbound* (1945) demonstrated his familiarity with the technicalities of psychoanalysis, a familiarity I shall be at pains to emphasize in this chapter.

Two crucial questions are refracted in the film script. When the murderer, Thorwald, confronts Jeffries at the climax of the film, he demands, "What do you want from me?" and when we are about to find out what Thorwald buried, then dug up, in the garden (discovered by the photographer's comparison to still slides), Stella cries, "I want no *part* of it." Jeffries unconsciously wanted to be the victim of Thorwald's sexual attack, in his homoerotic inversion of a Oedipal complex. And the buried part of Mrs Thorwald was her phallus, an imaginary item.

The neighbors on whom Jeffries peeps represent a panoply of sexual excitement and disillusionment: Miss Torso has many suitors and one hungry boyfriend; a newlywed couple move in but the wife is insatiable; a long-married couple sleep on their fire escape in opposite directions, Thorwald murders his constantly complaining wife, and a father dresses his little daughter on his fire escape, in a moment suggestive of displaced pedophilia. There are two frustrated women: one sculpts a figure with a large central empty hole, called "hunger," while the other, a suicidal "Miss Lonely-hearts", is saved at the last minute by the music of an unseen composer.

Lisa, who wants to marry Jeffries, also understands his psychology. She puts herself at risk by breaking into Thorwald's apartment while the photographer looks on like the enthralled viewer of a movie thriller, when Thorwald returned to catch her. He calls the police to rescue her after she finds Mrs. Thorwald's wedding ring. Jeffries sees it on her ring finger through his large telephoto lens (as if it were his erection). At one point, she threatens to get his attention by performing the Dance of the Seven Veils from Thorwald's apartment. In that allusion to the story of Salome (and John the Baptist) she fuses a Christian religious allusion with Jeffries' implied fascination with castration.

Blue Velvet makes the sexual implications of *Rear Window* explicit. The name of the protagonist, Jeff, is the most potent clue to their connection. The other analogs are more remote: For instance, the female stars of both films had very distinguished fathers and a Roman Catholic education: John B. Kelly Sr. was an Olympian gold medalist who was nearly elected Mayor of Philadelphia; Isabella Rossellini was the daughter of Roberto Rossellini (and Ingrid Bergman). The parallels are even more inverted in casting the male protagonists: James Stewart was the benign hero of many Hollywood films while Denis Hopper took on shadier roles. In *Blue Velvet* he plays a drug dealer and rapist. When Jeffrey, home from college because his father had a heart attack, finds a severed ear in a field, later he breaks into Dorothy Vallens' apartment to solve the crime himself. Like the photographer of *Rear Window* he peeps on her through the slates of her closet door. He sees Frank Booth (played by Hopper) who kidnapped her son and cut off her husband's ear, rape her. After Booth leaves Dorothy finds him and sexually abuses him. Thus, the latent fantasies of Hitchcock's film are materialized explicitly. Eventually Booth catches him in Dorothy's apartment, drags him to a bordello, kisses him and beats him. Throughout the film

Jeffrey keeps the company of Sandy Williams, a highschool girl he had picked up, whose father, a police detective, has put him on the scent of Booth, ironically by warning him to keep away from him. When Jeffrey and Sandy spot Dorothy, naked and beaten, on the street, Sandy's former highschool boyfriend, insultingly calls her Jeffrey's mother. I take this offhand allusion to incest to correspond to the father dressing his little daughter in *Rear Window*.

There is also a detective in Hitchcock's film, whose function is to throw cold water on the photographer's dire speculations. Furthermore, Dorothy's nightclub act features her singing Bobby Vinton's "Blue Velvet," analogous to the composer's song ("To See You is to Love You") and "Mona Lisa" heard in Hitchcock's film. There is even an implicit rhyme between Jeffries's discouragement of Lisa's affections by telling her of the horrible food he has to eat on his photographic assignments in the wild (while she has Club 21 cater their expensive meals) and a bird eating an insect to the horror of Jeffrey's aunt. The allusion to "disgusting" meals may actually be displacements of repressed homosexual oral intercourse. During the three decades between the films, the American commercial cinema had become much more liberal in the depiction of sexual activity. Hitchcock had so mastered the art of innuendo, that it is hard to imagine he would have thrived had he lived to make films in the Eighties or later.

Both films have epilogues. After his confrontation with Thorwald, who defenestrated him, Jeffries needed a new cast. By his side, Lisa surreptitiously substitutes a fashion magazine for the wildlife journal she was pretending to read before he fell asleep. *Blue Velvet* ends as Jeff's family holds a barbeque for Sandy and her parents, as if everything had returned to "normality."

Mosaik im Vertrauen [Mosaic in Trust]
and
The Falls

Peter Tscherkassy, the only useful critic of Peter Kubelk's *Mosaik im Vertrauen* (*Mosaic in Trust*, 1955), has summarized its action:

> *Mosaik im Vertrauen* has six characters: the railroad stationmaster, Johann Bayer; his young daughter; an Italian [sic; he is actually Yugoslavian] vagabond called Putnik (played by a fellow student from Rome); a Teddy Boy type named "Leo" in the end credits; the elegant lady Michaela; and her chauffeur, played by the poet Konrad Bayer.
>
> The plot is simple: Putnik spends his days in a railroad yard. From an appropriate distance he pines after the stationmaster's daughter. The stationmaster wants to drive the irksome hobo away. Additionally, Putnik is faced with the competition of Leo, who is also courting the stationmaster's daughter. Eventually, Michaela arrives on the scene, together with her chauffeur in a luxurious car. The latter remain silent observers as events unfold. They never interfere, though their arrival seems to have a negative influence on the course of things. One night around the campfire, Putnik and the stationmaster grow friendly. They get to talking and railroad man Bayer begins to tell a bit about his life. The men stay together till the light of dawn.
>
> The film ends with the departure of the Lady: The disc of the rising sun cuts to Michaela's broad-brimmed hat as she presses it to her head in the wake of the convertible's wind stream. As the end credits roll, the car disappears into the distance.

The film's editing is so disjunctive that it nearly emerges as a Menippean Satire on the erotic imagination in Vienna at the start of its post-WWII Modernism. Putnik, an immigrant spotted the young woman as she was hanging wash to dry. The first time he helps her take it off the lines, but the next morning, in a nearly identical scene, she refused his help, lest he soil the laundry.

In his wandering through the railroad yards the unnamed immigrant, played by Frederick Putnik, Kubelka's friend from the Centro Sperimentale di Cinematografia, enacts a most curious episode. After a moving camera shot of the railroad track, upside down and in reverse, he is seen looking at the tracks with his head between his legs. The curiosity stems from the fact, that unbeknownst to Kubelka (or his cameraman Ferry Radax) the American avant-garde cinema utilized the same trope over and over. In *Eyes Upside Down,* I cited the passage from Ralph Waldo Emerson's *Nature* (1836) as the touchstone for those American filmmakers. Kubelka surely had not read Emerson, whose text I quote on pp 149-150.

Intuitively, Kubelka had incorporated in his first film everything he could think of to disrupt its narrative. Thus, he had innocently hit upon the Emersonian topos. He also used newsreel footage of the 1955 Le Mans race accident, drawings, several silent color inserts into his black and white film – a red transistor radio, a woman's face, her fingernail on a new car tire, and a sunrise – while the soundtrack included several kinds of music, whistling, at least three languages (German, French and Italian are prominent) but necessarily fell silent for the color cut-ins. Much of the dialogue is in dialect. (Kubelka had been collecting fascinating phrases he overheard in the streets and shops of Austria. He called them "word rags.") Although it was taboo in Austrian commercial films, dialect played a major role in the avant-garde poetry of Kubelka's Austrian peers (the so-called Weiner Gruppe) with whom Radax associated and about whom he would eventually make TV films. The combined effect of the disjunctive sound, the rhythmic editing with its frequent repetitions of earlier images, and the fragments of speech in dialect, was to transform the film into a kaleidoscope of nearly autonomous scenes, thematically united to the failure of relations between men and women: The daughter of the stationmaster gives the same coy response to the immigrant and to Leo, a predatory dandy with a cigar and transistor radio; the stationmaster himself reduces marriage to a cup of coffee; the beautiful model, Michaela, steps out of her chauffeured car to a blasphemical parody, in Italian, of Jesus calling the dead Lazarus from the tomb in John's Gospel; her emergence seems to spark the tragedy at Le Mans by a slight of the editor's hand. Earlier the stationmaster had shouted to the immigrant to scram in the words, in German, that Jesus spoke to Lazarus's corpse, according to John's Gospel.

The suicided poet, Konrad Bayer, plays the chauffeur of his then girlfriend, Ida Szigethy, who was Michaela. Kubelka described Bayer's "distantiation" from others and from the world as like his own (Kubelka had proclaimed his succession from humanity at the age of nineteen), and he noted Bayer's genius for satire. The best introduction I know to the curious mentality of Vienna in the Fifties and to its sexuality would be Oswalt Weiner's brief essay "Some Remarks on Konrad Bayer: Dark Romanticism and Surrealism in Postwar Vienna."

The diversity of references, the radical scrambling of scenes, and the unfamiliar dialects combine to make *Mosaik im Vertrauen* nearly impenetrable without repeated viewings. Its initial effect resembles that of a favorite book for Kubelka; he loved James Joyce's *Ulysses* ever since he heard it disparaged by one of his teachers in Gymnasium. Each chapter of *Ulysses* is autonomous with its own style. (We would hardly know that the drunken Cyclops figure is the grandfather of Nausicaa figure were it not for the name of his dog. Likewise, I depend on Tscherkassyky's plot synopsis to know the stationmaster is the father of the young woman hanging washing.) Although there are no divisions within *Mosaik im Vertrauen*, several episodes or moments have distinct styles of editing. I have already mention the upside-down shots of the railroad tracks, The encounter of Leo with the Stationmaster's daughter is a rapidly edited fragment, situated between the two color shots of the radio and the woman's face; when the stationmaster changes an overhead light, but there are at least three long uninterrupted shots of the bulb; and near the end of the film there are night scenes with the stationmaster and the immigrant as they warm themselves by an open fire. There, the only interruption in the montage would be a color shot of a vehicle light, serving as a metaphor for the illumination of a lit cigarette. Eventually, the scene of the temporary reconciliation of the stationmaster and the immigrant morphs into the documentary shots of the winner at Le Mans, as the dawn breaks (in the final color insert). The repeated Biblical evocation "Veni fiori, Michaela" and the dandy's boast that the girl will fall ["verfallen" also repeated] for his routine of seduction stand out as if etched in the viewer's memory like the symmetrical design the immigrant scratched and drew on the side of a boxcar in the first shot (repeated at least twice more).

When Ken Kelman concluded his lecture series at the New York Filmmakers' Cinematheque with a talk on the films of Kubelka and Herbert Vessely, Kubelka vociferously expressed his disdain for Vessely. I know he hates the work of Peter Greenaway as intensely, so, this "incongruous" pairing will surely earn his contempt. Greenaway's first long film. *The Falls* (1980), is a genuine Menippean Satire while *Mosaik im Vertrauen* merely appears to be one because of its extreme fragmentation.

Sidney Peterson's ironic reduction of all cinematic soundtracks to either mood music or lip-synch might be applied to the cinematic version of Menippean satire the British Peter Greenaway refined and made his own with *The Falls*. The filmic Menippea in America has a somewhat longer history and at least two parallel tracks that do not intersect with each other: an avant-garde tradition with roots in the films of Peterson himself and Christopher MacLaine culminating in Hollis Frampton's *Hapax Legomena* (1971-72) and Michael Snow's *Rameau's Nephew* (1974);

and a vaudevillian strain of mainstream comedy that has comes through H.C. Potter's *Hellzapoppin'* [1941] to be massively dominated later by the filmmaking of Woody Allen. Greenaway's films show a clear influence of the former, little from the latter strain, but he has succeeded nevertheless in finding a place for his work in mainstream international production and distribution networks. In part, this success may have been abetted by the popularity of less demanding British Menippea, such as the Monty Python films. Yet a more significant factor seems to be Greenaway's wholly original assumption of the genius of British and Irish literary and fictional Menippea, the tradition of Fielding, Sterne, Swift, Smollett, and Richardson, into cinema. As we might expect, the more radical Greenaway films, those with which he began his filmic career, have benefited from the enthusiasm for his initial very stylish works that waned with his more conventional feature films, *The Draughtman's Contract* (1982), *Zed and Two Naught*s [or ZOO, 1985] *The Belly of the Architect* (1987), *Drowning by Numbers* (1988) *The Cook, The Thief, His Wife, and Her Lover* (1989), and *Prospero's Books* (1991).

Hollis Frampton (whose films Kubelka also disdains) woke up "one fine morning...to discover that, during the night, [he] had learned to understand the language of birds." That occasion could not have been later than 1972, when he confessed and expanded upon his revelation in the article "A Pentagram for Conjuring the Narrative," that he subsequently repudiated. There he shares with us what he understood to be the scope of avian discourse: "They say: 'Look at me!' or: 'Get out of here!' or: 'Let's fuck.' or: 'Help!' or: 'Hurrah!' or: 'I found a worm!' and that's 'all' they say." Then Frampton hastens to add, "And that, when you boil it down, is about all 'we' say." The homology between the discourse of birds and humans falls within his discussion on the omnipresence of narrative. In the same essay, in fact, merely a page before, describing the implicit hearer of any literary monologue, he suggested that even the most reductive narrative requires a second person, one "whose presence is felt only in the numbing quietude we normally expect of any discerning auditor forced to listen to a longwinded joke in poor taste..."

Peter Greenaway made a marvelous longwinded joke of filming *The Falls*, by arranging alphabetically the biographies of ninety-two of the purported nineteen million people who spontaneously learned bird languages, among other strange avian effects, as a result of the fictive Violent Unexplained Event (or VUE). One of those ninety-two (again) languages is called '*Hapax Legomena*,' surely in homage to the title of Frampton's first long serial film. The phrase is Greek, and as applied in classical philology, refers to a word that survives only in a single instance in Greek or Latin texts, thereby frustrating the lexicographical principle of comparing different usages to determine its meaning. Etymology and context are all philologists have to go on to read a 'hapax' or to determine if there has been a corruption in the manuscript transmission. For both Frampton and Greenaway the exploration of the autonomy and indeterminacy of language is a major task of cinema. In the same essay, Frampton playfully called the proposition that all films have a narrative, "Brakhage's Theorem." Brakhage returned the compliment several times by citing (and misquoting) the seven possible bird sentences as the full range of plots in narrative films.

When Greenaway paid homage to Frampton, acknowledging a colleague and precursor in the linguistically organized systemic film, he may have been at the same time slyly indicating a crucial difference between his work and Frampton's. If indeed Greenaway, through this obscure allusion, is inventing the fiction that Frampton too was a victim of the VUE when he learned the speech of birds, he implies that he mastered only how to speak and understand *Hapax Legomena*. Thus, unaware of the other ninety-one bird languages, Frampton mistook his egocentric limitations for the whole of bird-talk, a conclusion with which he may have been comfortable insofar as it confirmed his theory of human expression.

In any case, Greenaway is as much an English skeptic as

Frampton was an American heir to the Emersonian expansion of Selfhood. Although they shared a predilection for long systemic films, a fascination with the interventions of chance in art, and an ironic curiosity about all claims about the limitations of language, these two filmmakers diverged significantly on the centrality of the autobiographical impulse. Frampton mined high Modernism for the sources of cinematic form: Pound, Joyce, Borges and Beckett were his elective mentors; but in the end his cinema celebrates radical self-reliance and posits visionary schemes of perfected machines and idealized languages. Greenaway more elusively seems to have turned for inspiration to the Age of Samuel Johnson and the masters of 18th century English-language fiction. At every turn, he put into question the identities and claims of his characters and the authority of the narrative voice. His films are vehicles for arousing and compounding doubt, comedies with a cruel fascination for the varieties of mind/body dysfunctions.

Frampton's cinematic autobiography, (*nostalgia*), is the opening film of his seven-part *Hapax Legomena*. In it the camera never budged from its fixed stare at a hotplate as photographs were immolated in a chronological sequence, while we heard descriptions of them and of their relevance to the filmmaker's life. But the descriptions were displaced: We would hear them just before we see the images. *The Falls* is nearly as monomorphic and repetitive as (*nostalgia*). But it hides it brilliantly. The sheer piling up of ninety-two biographies in alphabetical order questions the nature and authority of any diachronic account of a life, especially one marked by a mythic catastrophe. Like Frampton's filmic autobiography, the voiceover narration gives meaning to the bland images. As a technical feat *The Falls* is a dazzling transformation of diverse seascapes, lakes, and landscapes, talking heads, still photographs, the recitation of bird names, a few archival film clips, and songs into a hilariously labyrinthine "mockumentary" of mysterious evidence and false clues to an absurd fiction.

The VUE gradually appears to be an allegory of the Freudian Unconscious, with scattered elements of incest, (Oedipal) blindness, murder, obsessions, bestiality, dreams, flight fantasies, primal scenes, and parapraxes. At the same time the film constitutes a comic parody of all those Freudian commonplaces.

In the biography of Affracious Fallows (the seventy-fifth in the series), we find an allegory of both the filmmaker and the characteristic viewer of *The Falls*: Affracious, a school-headmaster before the VUE, suffered a number of physical aberrations, including "enlarged genitalia," lost his position and was reduced to odd jobs including "occasional prostitution," Latin tutoring, and bird identification. In the biography, we hear that the car he is seen driving around a traffic circle several times was "stolen" and that he celebrated the thirteenth anniversary of the VUE robbing insignificant objects (an umbrella, earrings, shoes, etc.) from a number of summer cottages around Abersoch on the Lleyn Peninsula in Wales (a locale so often mentioned in the film that it becomes one of many running gags) in order to be arrested; for the initial letters of the names of the cottages spelled "Hoopoe," his totem bird; while the initial letters of the words for the stolen objects spelled its Latin name "Upupa Epops," and the start of the names of the cottage owners spelled "Affracious." The narrative catalogue of thefts accompanies a montage of photographs and film shots of cottages, owners, and recovered objects, labelled as exhibits by the Abersoch police. Finally, a chart of the anagrams appears on the screen, considerably extended, as we hear that the Abersoch police could not relinquish their anagrammatic detection once they were "put on the track." That would reflect the critical miscalculations of writers such as myself.

Greenaway's inane associations of objects, places, and names are implanted in his film in order to be detected, but like the Abersoch police, we will never know how far to let the process take us. Is it relevant to note that the catalogue of names from Orchard Falla (1) to Anthior Fallwaste (92) brackets the film between a garden and a devastation, reflecting the Book which guides Christian lives? Surely, the cabalistic clues of Affracious are more farfetched. Was the student in a seminar on cinematic comedy going too far when he read Corntopia Fallas (19) as an etymology and a pun: horn-place phallus, or the phallus in the place of the cuckold, and then noted the emphasis on "woodcock" and a series of "tits" in her recorded bird list? Or does the film sanction such gender confusions by referring to VUE victims as, for instance, "a middle-aged female man," (26) an oddity eventually explained in the biography of Canopy Fallbenning (34) as the "sexual quadromorphism" of many VUE victims. Perhaps even the saint's and surnames of the filmmaker can be interpreted as "causes" for the film's obsessive neurosis: Greenaway is a metonym for "Fall" as the season when the disappearance of chlorophyll transforms the landscape; and 'Peter' has been a euphemism for penis since 1902.

Certain themes permeate the biographies almost from the beginning of the film: the origins of the VUE are unknown but somehow associated with birds or flight; victims usually speak at least one bird language, often suffer minor avian metamorphoses of parts of the body and tend toward an obsession with some aspect of the disaster, very commonly dreaming of water. Many of them, like Affracious, favor circular movement; so that we see small planes circling on the ground at an airport, a truck driving circles on the beach, a van limited to circling in a park, and of course, cars making 360-degree turns.

Following perhaps Freud's suggestion of the links between paranoia and the elaboration of philosophical systems, Greenaway introduces another dimension of doubt by having his creatures offer a range of theories about the malevolent nature of the event from the widely held idea of "The Responsibility of Birds" to the scoffed-at idea of ratite revenge. He also periodically mentions the reputed secret society, FOX, the Society For Ornithological Extermination, whose van with a NID license plate and the word CROW on its side ran down Bwythan and Vacete Fallbutus (41, 45). Among the numerous conspiracy theories about the origins of the VUE, that of Obsian Fallicut (68) stands out: initially convinced it was a hoax to promote Hitchcock's *The Birds*, Obsian develops a paranoid fascination with cinema, eventually leaving his job in a film laboratory to emigrate to Hollywood where he edits The Hoopoe, a journal about birds in feature films, covertly funded by the Hitchcock estate. This is one of the many instances in which filmmaking, as well as viewing, cataloguing, and preserving films, gets caught in *The Falls*'s skeptical labyrinth. In a sense, the disaster occurred only to become a film – or a series of films insofar as the narrators of *The Falls* promise, or threaten, updated versions of it. Thus, the archaic human aspiration to fly conjoins with the perhaps equally ancient desire to represent motion as ultimate sources of the repetitive tendency to fall from any form of contentment with human limitations. Airplanes and film paraphernalia became foci of obsessions in the depicted lives, as if the secret of fallenness could be found in the recent technological products of a fallen imagination.

The skeptical gnostic artist, manipulating and seemingly extending endlessly *The Falls*, offers moments of relief from its delicious tedium when he throws out one or another of the ninety-two lives, because of a legal complication or an error discovered in the Directory, as when Erek Fallfree (63) is excluded because his biography is under exclusive contract to "Crow Films," or in the mistake that produced Joyan Fallicory (66): a place name, Fallicory, was wrongly attributed to a VUE victim who should be found in the Directory under Joy; or, above all, when bogus reasons are adduced for excluding Agostina Fallmutt and Castan Fallockery (72, 73) to disguise the producers' anxiety that those lives are too lengthy to be included. Here as often elsewhere in the film, we seem closer to the world of Monty Python than Hollis Frampton. All through the film verbal misunderstandings, such as hearing "Blessed are the cheesemakers," (instead of "peacemakers") in *The Life of Brian* (1979), take on virtually theological force.

The closest the filmmaker actually comes to articulating the gnostic theology of his encyclopedia of fallenness is in the jeremiad of the perpetually eighty-three-year-old Canopy Fallbenning who calls the God of the VUE a "charlatan," an "inexperienced quack," eventually softening the accusation to a God who has "lost an essential skill." More indirectly Bwythan Fallbutus (41) suggests a more orthodox punishment by entitling his book on VUE languages The View from Babel. Conversely, nothing is made of the Christian symbol of the bird as a figure for the Holy Ghost. Greenaway's fallen world has no hint of redemption. There is not even an allusion, so far as I can detect, to the film's cinematic counterpart, Pasolini's Uccellacci e uccellini (1966), which elaborately plays with Christian bird/ angel symbolism.

As we make our way through the film, a number of characters whose names do not begin with the letters F-A-L-L, loom out of the penumbra of the nonstop narrations: several victims have favorite stories by Tulse Luper, the "master strategist and cataloguer" of the VUE; there are repeated references to Rapper Begol, the second custodian of the "Boulder Orchard" on the Lleyn Peninsula, one of the epicenters of the VUE – (the other is the Goldhawk Road in West London); a filmmaker and another onetime Custodian of the "Boulder Orchard," H.E. Carter, whose film of water we see, dedicated "in happy remembrance of many wet dreams" to the hilariously freakish squirter Aptesia Fallarme (18) the "human waterfall;" and the ornithologist Van Hoyten of the Amsterdam Zoo. In part, the experience of watching The Falls entails piecing together parts of an incomplete puzzle that leads to other Greenaway films, such as A Walk Through H: The Reincarnation of an Ornithologist [1979] about Tulse Luper as well as the late multi-media project Tulse Luper's Suitcases [2003-2011]} or ZOO, where Van Hoyten plays a major role.

Yet, by far the most absorbing system of references interweaves aspects of the ninety-two biographies. The arbitrary selection of names of victims beginning with F-A-L-L had been abetted, we learn in the story of Corntopia Fallas (19), by the fortunately prescient decision of future victim Erhaus Bewler Falluper (88) to make a filmed survey of bird knowledge of people listed in the same public registry as himself (seven of whom became VUE victims, whose interviews, made eighteen months before the event, are incorporated into the film). These films are so silly, that the possibility that the VUE was revenge for such a waste of film cannot be wholly dismissed.

The clustering of F-A-L-L names naturally entails an assortment of married couples and relatives. Early in the film the elusive Standard Fallaby (5) cannot be found: as the camera rolls past numerous nearly identical trailer homes. We hear that Standard, a speaker of Curdine, the bird language of ambiguities and puns, hides his trailer to avoid the incestuous advances of his sister, Tasida Fallaby (6), whom we then see nude, reading from her autobiography, laboriously written in Curdine which she imperfectly learned to communicate with Standard, and thus composed with considerable "unconscious innuendo." In the autobiography, she claimed to have been born holding her brother's hand, although her birth certificate asserted she was two years older.

The false twins Ipson and Pulat Fallari (16), born simultaneously of twin sisters and one father, were pilots whose twin-like relationship was disrupted by Ipson's marriage to Stachia Fallari (17), who had become Van Hoyten's mistress by the time of the VUE (which further alienated the brothers by giving them virtually opposite bird languages). Making the web even more intricate, one of the voiceover narrators refers to Tulse Luper's fictionalized life of the brothers (which may even be the very film biography we are watching).

The most striking visual thread in this essentially verbal tapestry links the widely scattered use of newsreel footage of flying stunts and primitive flying contraptions, above all images of a man with a faulty parachute on the Eiffel Tower. The first reference to the leaper who died in the attempt to fly occurs in the second biography, that of Constance Ortuist Fallaburr, who maintained that the flyer was Nathan Isolde Demontelier and that he jumped from the Eiffel Tower in 1870. When her husband, flight-historian Melorder Fallaburr (3), argued that this was impossible because the Eiffel Tower was built in 1889, she claimed he must have jumped from the roof of Les Invalides. The first actual images of the leaper appear in the biography of the singer and composer Musicus Fallantly (12) who dedicated his choral song in Welsh and the bird language Allo to Demontelier; but Fallantly claimed the man was the French linguist and baritone, Van Richert, and that he jumped in 1889. However, his wife, Cadence, not a VUE victim, pointed out that in that case the film must be a reconstruction because the cinema was not invented until 1895. The same teasing shot of the man on the Eiffel Tower shows up in the life of the "gifted petomane" Vacete Fallbutus (45) because of his identification with the heroic Richfelt who is said to have jumped to his death in 1909. When the Fallbutus family scorned the idea of his ascending the Eiffel Tower because of Vacete's acrophobia, he is said to have jumped from a railway bridge only to be run over by the Crow van. The image reappears, without comment, in the story of Obsian Fallicutt (68), but it is not until the life of Crasstranger Fallqueue (78) that we finally see the shocking fall from the tower. Preceded by droll images of would-be flyers, roller-skating with wings tied to their arms, and a man bathing nude in an airborne tub – the Fallqueues were air-acrobats – the teasing parachute seems comic before it turns horrifying, as the leaper hits the pavement at the foot of the tower. As a flight historian of acknowledged accuracy, Crasstranger has the final word on the identity of the dead man: the Austrian clothing manufacturer Reichert, who died in 1911, demonstrating a parachute uniform he had designed. He was the only victim discussed in connection with the fall who was not contradicted by a relative, perhaps because he was a sole survivor of a persecuted, and regularly defenestrated, family.

The newsreel images are the only spectacular visual elements in the whole film. Greenaway's most impressive achievement is the transformation of hours of otherwise pedestrian images into a fascinating narrative. He intercuts the talking heads of several narrators with slides, still photographs, and charts; musical performances (predominately by solo singers), book illustrations, landscapes, written words, seascapes, and cityscapes, both static and filmed from moving vehicles; details of airplanes, bathtubs, kites, elevators, toys, etc.; and bits of films projected on walls, screens, and running through editing machines. The narrations are often continued by several talking heads, and frequently are superimposed as English translations over barely audible speeches in European or made-up bird languages; in one case a man speaking Dutch interviews Appis (Arris) Fallabus (4) who responds in Pig Latin (also known here as Dog and Hog Latin). The dense melodic landscape is further enhanced by a sound-mix of waves, dripping faucets, and other water sounds, the cries of birds, songs, and complex musical interventions.

The individual biographies can be elaborate montages or even a single shot: Cash Fallbaez (28) is illustrated by a static image of the overturned car in the rural landscape where he died; one tracking shot of mobile homes accompanies the narrative of Standard Fallaby's seclusive biography; a single zoom starts from the mouth of the singer Pollie Fallory (74) and slowly reveals her standing before the microphone into which she sings.

Between each life there is a passage of a blank screen with the name and number printed on it. The same infectious musical phrase marks the beginning of each unit. Michael Nyman's score is one of the glories of the film. It underlines the dramatic, melodramatic, nostalgic, and grotesque convolutions of the narratives. The chanting of the bird names in the VUE anthem becomes addictive in its well-placed repetitions. The score's sparseness is consistent with the visual style of the film.

Here is an example of Greenaway's brilliant use of minimal materials: in the hilarious life of Coppice Fallbateo (30) we see only the talking heads of three narrators and a slide of Piero della Francesca's *Brera Virgin*, with a panning movement to its suspended egg. The commentators describe the mutilated art historian Coppice's failed attempt to learn the VUE language Betelgeuse, with its rapidly shifting diction, and his subsequent success at seducing his Betelgeuse-speaking art student, Aldona Perdone, by failing her and offering private tutoring even though her copy of the painting was "considerably better" than Piero's original. In the stages of their brief relationship "Aldona" (in Betelgeuse) meant successively "yellow," "yolk," and "embryo." At the time of the birth of their child, Piero dell'Adona, it meant "egg."

The imaginative fecundity and the elaborate wit of the deadpan text that underlies the biographies transforms and enlivens the mundane visual information, as if demonstrating Hollis Frampton's assertion, in "Film in the House of the Word," that "language, in every culture, and before it may become an arena of discourse, is, above all, an expanding arena of power, claiming for itself and its wielders all that it can seize, and relinquishing nothing."

But in that same essay Frampton posits "two hypothetical symbolic systems[:]...a universal natural language ...[and]... a perfect machine," so that "a consequent celestial mechanics of the intellect might picture a body called Language, and a body called Film, in symmetrical orbit about one another, in perpetual dialectical motion." For Greenaway, it would seem, such a visionary project is as foolish and hubristic as either the catastrophic desires for flight or perfect representation. He repeatedly subverts his narrative by hinting that the characters of *The Falls* (or its near homonym, "The False") invented their own film, and that the VUE is 'UNKNOWN' because it is "unknowable," a non-event. Three montage-films by Anteo Fallasby (20), an "inventor of fictitious languages" including the regularly mentioned Hartelese B take up biographies 20, 22, and 23, planting, early-on, the suggestion that Anteo may have made the film we are watching. (Fifty-five lives later we learn that Affracious Fallows was paroled a year before his sentence was up for permitting his mouth to be reconstructed so he could speak Hartelese B.) Bewick Fallcaster (48) is said to be collecting music for "an encyclopedic work of biography." Presumably he stands in for Michael Nyman, who composed his remarkable score from variations on Mozart's K.364 and pieces by Brian Eno; the former might be crudely associated with the sweet ritornello we hear again and again especially over the images of a pastoral landscape and lake surfaces in the life of Wrallis Fallanway (13) who is said to have drowned in "artificial Lake Eleven;" while the gallop (to use the dichotomy of Deleuze) might be identified with the short series of notes over the titles introducing each biography, as well as in the throbbing melody heard with the images of the boulders in the Orchard.

As the film draws toward its end, the internal references become more emphatic: Erhaus Bewler Falluper (88) (whose name veers suspiciously close to Tulse Luper's) is said to have been capable of inventing the VUE and more pointedly to be someone who "doesn't know the difference between a good joke and a bad one." Castral Fallvernon (90) turns out to be the archivist who collects the photographs used in the film, while Leasting Fallvo (91), also said to have been able to have invented the VUE, has supplied the VUE library with a number of fictions, whose titles would fit several of the film's biographies, including "The Making of Hartelese B" and "Bird Tales of the Eiffel Tower."

Although *The Falls* shares a narrative exuberance and structural complexity with such fictions as Georges Perec's *Life: A User's Manual*, its more direct literary affinities are classical. In Aristophanes' 'Birds', the political aspirations of imperialist Athens are refracted through Pisthetairos' self-transformation into a bird, with the collaboration of his precursor, the Hoopoe; he leads the birds in a successful challenge of the gods' supremacy over the universe. From Ovid, Greenaway seems to have derived his humorous attention to the often-painful details of physical metamorphoses.

The opening credits of the film appear over images of large

stones, filmed in black and white by a someone walking with a hand-held camera. A few trees may be glimpsed in the landscape and a barn in the distance, but the camera remains close to the rocks, weaving between and around them. This will turn out to be, presumably, the Boulder Orchard of the Tyddyn-Corn farm on the Lleyn peninsula near the towns of Botwinnog and Abersoch, although it is not specifically identified as such until the black and white footage reappears in fragments illustrating the biography of Vasian Falluper (87) who "claims to have discovered in the disposition of the rocks and trees and intricate system of passageways that, in miniature, matched both the pilgrim tracks of the Lleyn peninsula and the known routes of migrational birds in the Northern Hemisphere."

Visions of the Boulder Orchard recur in the biographies of Starling Fallanx (15) where an inserted 8mm film reel shows her and her sister playing there as children. Catherine Fallbutus occupied the farm with her two daughters at the time of the VUE. Her biography (42) presents us with views of the farmhouse, its fields, and the Boulder Orchard (accompanied as usual with the throbbing gallop). In biography 57 Agrimany Fallchester illegally collects souvenirs from the Boulder Orchard for sale. The very term "Boulder Orchard" is an oxymoron, perfectly suited to the self-abolishing rhetoric of *The Falls*.

The grab-bag genre of the Menippean Satire indirectly hits at a variety of targets. *The Falls*, at its core, is a parody of an inconclusive science-fiction narrative about a mysterious, potentially toxic, landscape on the Lleyn peninsula. Every time we glimpse it, a narrow range of dramatic music underlines its mystery. One major film that *The Falls* spoofs might be Andrei Tarkovsky's *Stalker* (1979) where the mysterious "Zone" allegorizes the powers of a site of nuclear spill. There is a hint of nuclear disaster in the recurrent references to ninety-two languages, biographies, etc. insofar as the atomic number of uranium is 92.

Yet, there are many segments of *The Falls* that cast doubt on the role of the Boulder Orchard in the VUE. Late in the film the range of magical landscapes widen to include "the grounds of Fountains Abbey near Ripon, Yorkshire" (77) and the Black Forest (79). In the former, the narrative account of Sallis Fallpino's experience links proximity to the Neoclassical Temple of Piety to an increased "Carthaganian vocabulary and... greater... weight-loss." In the Black Forest, Romanese Fallracce was struck by lightning the morning of the VUE. His celebrity appearances lead audiences to attribute the cause of the event to an electrical excess rather than the vengeance of birds. Just as the text by itself imparts mystery to the elegant lawn, pond, and pseudo-temple of Fountain Abbey, an ominous high-pitched inarticulate singing voice – the typical cue that sites in sci-fi films are threatening – goes along with images of the Fallracce family driving along a firebreak amid the forest's pines.

The theory and practice of what Deleuze and Guattari called melodic landscapes is close to the explicit subject of the biography of Geoffrey Fallthuis (83), a purported filmmaking pupil of Tulse Luper "who supported the Luper program for an unassisted natural landscape" by shooting a film of a wych elm on the south bank of the Thames before it was cut down to make room for the Royal Festival Hall. He edited the film to the microrhythms of Anton Webern's *Five Pieces for Orchestra*, op. 10, which appears intermittently throughout the biography. He was in Toronto, Canada at the time of the VUE, but nevertheless he suffered from its characteristic metamorphoses. Upon returning to the locale of his unfinished film when his wife, Corntopia Felixchange, was singing at the London opera, he suspiciously fell to his death, perhaps murdered, in a situation faintly echoing the demise of Webern himself who was accidentally shot by an American soldier while smoking on his balcony in 1945.

Fallthuis's short film is an excellent parody of an avant-garde effort at visual music. By focusing on a tree isolated amid the new constructions of the Thames' south bank, it bridges the imaginary urban and rural epicenters of the VUE. Finally, Fallthuis's death by accident or murder belies an ambivalent and inconsistent benefit of VUE victimage: immortality because of the cessation of aging. The only termination of a VUE victim's life would be burial under a "bird-scarer" (or more familiarly, a "scarecrow.") So, at the end of the catalogue, all we see in the final ninety-second biography is a whirling scarecrow, as we hear that Anthior Fallwaste has "successfully terminated a relationship with birds." Except for the chanting of the VUE anthem of bird names over the final credits, *The Falls* falls silent.

Rashomon (1950).

Mr Hulot's Holiday (1953).

Rear Window (1954).

Blue Velvet (1986).

The Falls (1980).

Mosaic In Trust (1955).

Marnie
and
Il deserto rosso [The Red Desert]

Before *The Wizard of Oz* did it in 1939, dozens of films combined color footage with black and white. Andrei Tarkovsky filmed the frame story of *Stalker* in sepia color but the scenes in The Zone in vivid colors. Two films, shot entirely in color, remarkable for their thematic use of chroma are *Marnie* and *Il deserto rosso* (*The Red Desert*), both made in 1964.

Psychoanalytical criticism has something to tell us about films made by men about women with sexual problems. In this chapter I have brought together these two films because of their striking use of color in portraying frigid female protagonists; and I believe both marshal Freudian ideas to pinpoint their sexual problems with coming-of-age maturity as manifested in menstruation. Of course, neither film is as explicit in this as Brian De Palm's vulgar horror film, *Carrie* (1976).

Marnie makes no bones about its psychoanalytical source: at a confessional moment Marnie herself parodies the classic couch situation by fusing it with the mythos of Tarzan, saying to her inquiring husband, Mark Rutland, with whom she cannot have sex, "You Freud, Me Jane." Eventually Rutland uncovers the origin of her neurosis: she killed a sailor while he was having sex with her prostitute mother. The mother took the full blame and went to prison, where she became an super-devout Christian. The flashback revelation of the murder "explains" the earlier scenes in which Marnie reacted in horror to blood and to red ink. It also accounts for her compulsive thefts and attempts to secure her mother's love with money and costly presents.

The film ends with an optimistic suggestion that Marnie will eventually overcome her affliction. But the eponymous novel by Winston Graham that Hitchcock adapted concludes with one of her robbery victims organizing a gang rape to punish Marnie. Hitchcock added the allusions to psychoanalysis, thereby banalizing the psychology of the novel. In essence, he returned to the tongue-in-cheek version of superficial psychoanalysis he made the center of his previous evocation of Freudian clichés, *Spellbound* (1945), and to Hollywood's theory of trauma as universally founded on terrible violence.

Films that have made sophisticated use of color are very rare. Carl Th. Dreyer knew this in 1955 when he distinguished between genuine 'color films' and the banal prevalence of 'colored films.' When color was not the norm, a few extraordinary artists made highly innovative color films. Michelangelo Antonioni's *Il deserto rosso* is one of the finest examples in the entire history of cinema: he employed a shift of color film stock to emphasize the imaginative power of an idyllic landscape (along with the Siren lure of strange sounds). *Il deserto rosso* used much more subtly (and without explicitly mentioning psychoanalysis) many of the same ideas Hitchcock more crudely deployed.

In my 1995 book, *Vital Crises in Italian Cinema*, I analyzed the film in terms of its reworking of motifs from Dante's *Inferno* and *Purgatorio* and their political implications. Here I wish to amplify that analysis in the light of psychoanalysis. In doing so, I shall be far from original. Ever since the film was shown, viewers have referred to the relevance of psychoanalytical discourse to it. When it won the Golden Lion at the 1964 Venice Film Festival, Luigi Chiarini, the festival director, referred to the entire array of films in competition as the year of "cinema post-psicoanalitico." Despite the half century of attention to this matter, there remain crucial details that have never been examined.

Within the stylistic fabric of Antonioni's meticulously crafted cinematic palette for his first, and most refined, color film, there is a seven-minute passage filmed on conventionally vivid color filmstock that stands out from the rest of the work by its sheer contrast and because it illustrates a story the protagonist, Giuliana, tells her son, when she imagines he is sick with polio (or he is faking the disease). Its fifty-four shots are considerably shorter than most of those of the film in which it is embedded.

The plot of *Il deserto rosso* revolves around a neurotic or perhaps even psychotic protagonist, the wife of a supervisor in petrochemical factory in Ravenna, during the few days that Corrado, the owner of the plant, visits to recruit workers for his new factory in Patagonia. During those days he seduces Giuliana, who is recuperating from a suicide attempt. The eccentric use of color throughout the film refracts Giuliana's aberrant vision and her obsession with pollution and disease: fruit denuded of chroma, yellow poisonous gasses shooting from smokestacks, the camera tracking along electric blue guidelines on the factory wall, etc.

The following revised quotation from *Vital Crises in Italian Cinema* will provide the gist of my thinking on the film:

> All around Giuliana are the visible marks of pollution and the signs of disease. A ship bearing a flag of quarantine enters the harbor; her son pretends to have contracted polio, to her panic. Giuliana's own mode of rhetoric fuses fantasy with self-revelation as she tells her son a story, illustrated by a brilliant shift of color tones. Thus, into this film of murky colors in short focus, Antonioni introduces an episode in the conventional color of a travelogue with a play of deep and shallow focus, made striking by contrast to the rest of the film. The story Giuliana tells her son is evidently a fantasy of her own pre-adolescence, in an environment with none of the hellish impurities and disease she perceives or imagines around her…
>
> The bedside story deserves close attention in itself and in its place-ment in the film. The sexuality of the fictive girl, always alone on the island, is emphasized by the narrative – that she does not like boys or

adults – and by the *uncommented visual detail* of her taking off the top of her two-piece bathing suit as she leaves the beach. In a way she too is a child version of …Diana, in an enchanted paradise with birds and wild rabbits. But her serenity is disturbed by the arrival of a phantom ship and the subsequent disembodied female voice singing to lure her to explore a cove where she suddenly realizes that the rocks resemble flesh. Consequently, interwoven in her story are elements of the Flying Dutchman and Odysseus' encounter with the Sirens. Like Senta in Wagner's opera and Odysseus, she is attracted by forces that would lead to her destruction…The story seems to have a therapeutic effect on her son, who "regains" the use of his legs after hearing it. But this magical effect is actually another indication that his illness had been Giuliana's imaginative projection, and that by recounting the fantasy she has overcome the compulsion to project the image of disease and arrested growth on her son. But unlike the healthy psychological use of fairy tales Bruno Bettleheim describes in *The Uses of Enchantment*, Giuliana's story merely shifts her compulsive behavior; for the story apparently reawakens her need for erotic sacrifice, propelling her in a panic to the hotel room of Corrado, an Odysseus-like seducer…. The story is further linked to the culmination of the seduction by a verbal parallel. In answer to Valerio's question, "who was singing?" she said "tutti," everyone and everything. When Corrado asks what she fears, she concludes her catalogue with "everything: the streets… the factories… the colors… the sky… the people… everything."

As she tells the story of the girl on the island, and as we see it on the screen, the synchronization between her words and the images suggests that what she is saying calls up the things and events we see. At first, no sooner does she say "cormorants," "seagulls", or "wild rabbits" than we see separate shots of each creature. When she mentions the 'pink sand' of the beach slightly before we see it, her description alerts us to notice the color.

Here is a literal translation of what Giuliana says in the Italian voice-over while the fantasy or memory unrolls on the screen:

> There was a girl who lived on an island. Being with adults disturbed her; they frightened her. Kids of her own age didn't please her anymore because they played at being adults, so she was always alone… with the cormorants, the seagulls, and the wild rabbits.
> She discovered a little beach far from the land where the sea… She really liked that place. There, nature had such beautiful colors, and

ODD COUPLES + 106

there was never any noise. She would leave as the sun was setting.

One morning she spotted a sail. Usually, the passing ships were very different. But this one was a real sailing vessel, the kind that crossed all the seas in the world, and, who knows?; beyond the world. Seen from afar it had a splendid effect. But seen a bit closer, it became mysterious. Who was steering it? There seemed to be no one on board. It would stop for a few minutes, then begin to come about, and then silently move away.

The girl was used to the weirdness of adults and wasn't very surprised. But when she went back to the shore, then, guess what? [ecco che] ... One mystery is ok, but two are too much! Who was singing? The beach was deserted, as it always is, but yet there was a voice... now there, now far away. For a minute it seemed that it had been coming from out of the sea itself... a cove between the rocks... so many rocks that... hadn't she noticed?... were like flesh. and at that moment the voice was very gentle.

Fabrizio: But who was singing?

Everything was singing... everything... [The ellipses indicate breaks in her narration, not omissions.]

A significant shift occurs between the shot of her leaving the beach, topless, and the next image of her entering the frame from the right, wearing both pieces of an apparently different bathing suit – of a lighter maroon color. The momentary oddity of the cut is explained almost immediately when, fifteen seconds later, Giuliana's "una mattina" ['one morning'] indicates that an indeterminate time has passed between the two shots. (It may well be that she was wearing the same bathing suit if it looked darker when it was wet; in the morning it was dry and would seem to be of a lighter tone.)

At this point, it is as if her language had to keep up with her mental images. At the start of the episode, the synchrony and slight anticipation might be said to place the viewer in the imaginary position of her son, who would have had to picture what we were seeing on the basis of her words; but now it is as if we were sharing her pictorial imagination or memory as she was in the act of finding words to portray her mental images to her son.

Such flexibility of perspective led Pier Paolo Pasolini to make

Il deserto rosso his prime example of the adaptation of free indirect discourse to cinema. In literature the free indirect style allows the fluid passage back and forth from subjective to omniscient narration. Giuliana employs it for the first time in her voiceover when she asks, neither herself nor Fabrizio, "Who was steering [the ghost ship]?" The three jump cuts of the departing vessel elliptically confirm the blending of perspectives. Her words "ecco che" that I have crudely rendered 'Guess what?' are further instances of free indirect discourse, as is the question 'who was singing?' The wordless soprano voice, as manifestly audible to the viewers as the other sounds – the lapping of waves, the wind, various bird songs – is simultaneously objective and subjective in this context: for us, it is on the same ontological level as all the other elements of the story, just as it would be for the boy; but at the same time, if it is either a genuine mystery or a psychological aberration, it must be heard as an auditory hallucination for the girl (and implicitly for Giuliana as she recounts it). The final sentences of the voiceover do more than confirm what may or may not strike the perceptive viewer: that the weathered rocks look like massings of human 'flesh.' They indicate that this was the telos to which the entire story was aiming, that that recognition was a milestone in her life or in the life of the girl she was inventing to soothe her son. The mystical response that 'tutti' were singing constitutes a thematic acknowledgement of the magical fusion latent throughout the story.

Antonioni himself has offered a strikingly naïve or deliberately misleading view of the episode when he told *Hunanité dimanche* (Sept. 13, 1964):

> ...there was only one scene in which I used color "normally"... It is the scene in which Giuliana having run out of stories in which to tell her sick son makes one up with great simplicity and purity of heart. In that sequence, the plot is suspended as if the eye and the conscience of the narrator had been distracted elsewhere. In fact, that sequence, in which each element – first of all, color – tells a fragment of the human experience, shows reality as Giuliana wishes it were – , that is, different from the world that appears to her as transformed, alien-

ated, obsessive to the point of being monstrously deformed.

The filmmaker says nothing here of the oneiric quality of the episode, and merely implied his protagonist's identification with the girl when he says it "shows reality as [she] wishes it were." But the intricate play of synchronization between the voiceover and the remarkable montage of long and telephoto shots (taken by two cameras shooting at once) is not the only indication of the care with which the sequence was conceived and constructed. Two images manifestly reveal the contrivance at work in its execution. The first would be the fifth shot of the sequence in which a rabbit rushes along the shore's edge and becomes totally soaked by the water before crawling out. Whereas it might have been very easy to capture the two previous shots – of a swimming cormorant, and a gull perched on a rock before it flies off – no cameraman would be lucky enough to film a rabbit running into and out of the water, with a massive 35mm camera already set in place on its steady mount. That shot had to be set up; the animal released and filmed. It is very likely that Antonioni had to make several attempts, perhaps even using several rabbits, to get those four seconds into the finished film. Perhaps the iconographic significance of the rabbit motivated the contrivance. Antonioni, a painter himself, would know those works in which Piero di Cosimo, Titian, Pinturicchio, Ghirlandaio, Pisanello and others painted rabbits and hares as symbols of fertility, vitality, and sometimes lust. Other elements may, or may not be, iconographic. I can think of no place where seagulls so function, although in *Paradise Lost*, Satan disguised himself as a cormorant to enter Eden before tempting Eve.

The morning of the appearance of the mysterious ship begins with the girl kneeling to smell a white flower. If it is actually a *Narcissus poeticus*, its name contributes a further autoerotic tonality to the island fantasy. Traditionally, the rabbit is Venus's pet. Within this little episode, the way that rabbit is thrust, or thrusts itself, onto the beach and into and out of the water forecasts the sudden appearance and disappearance of the ghost ship; and they both reflect Corrado's entry and imminent departure from Giuliana's sphere.

The other deliberately contrived image has already been mentioned: the naked torso of the girl seen from the back. No child of that age would casually take off the top of her two-piece swimming outfit in front of a film crew, even with her back turned, unless commanded to do so. The tan line itself attests to her modesty.

In *Vital Crises in Italian Cinema* (1995) I proposed, without demonstration or argument, a psychoanalytically inflected interpretation of the story. when I wrote:

> Yet it is also a story of the awakening of her sexuality, implicitly collapsing the oncoming of menstruation with the loss of cleanliness and clarity… Like Senta in Wagner's opera and Odysseus, she is attracted by forces that would lead to her destruction. We already know that Giuliana is recovering from an automobile accident, and it seems likely, from one of her stories to Corrado, that she had actually attempted suicide, as Marnie did in Hitchcock's nearly contemporaneous film. Thus, in her story, sexual awakening is confused with the magical ideas of erotic self-sacrifice and the quest for hidden experience and knowledge.
>
> From early in the film we know that her "accident" has left many traces, among them her frigid refusal of her husband's sexual overtures. In the chain of associations in this "post-psichoanalitico" film, pollution and sexuality are confused. Her fantasies of the prepubescent moment evoke a pristine, ecologically harmonious landscape, but that very evocation ineluctably contains the excitement and fascination of an eroticized world of mystery, desire, and flesh.

Not coincidentally, one of the finest psychoanalytic studies of a film ever published in English reveals the undercurrents of Antonioni's subsequent film, *Blow Up* (1965), a film *in color* in the merely conventional, decorative sense, according to Carl Dreyer's distinction. Also, not coincidentally, Jacob Arlow, in that brilliant study of "The Revenge Motive in the Primal Scene," pays no attention to the strategies of framing and editing that distinguish *Blow Up* from banal variants on its plot. Consequently, by ignoring the exquisite, elliptical montage of the protagonist blowing up photographs he took of what might be a murder and arranging them sequentially and spatially, as if they were stills from a film, Arlow overlooks the implicit plea of Antonioni that his own neurosis [a primal scene disturbance, according to Arlow's utterly convincing analysis] must be tied to the source of his creativity – the filmmaking process in which the primal scene disturbance is sublimated into poetic fascination and discovery in art.

My surmise that the emphasis and shift in the tonality and lucidity of *Il deserto rosso*'s color was related to menstruation occurred before I looked into the psychoanalytical literature that I shall quote below. The primary impulse to write this brief essay, and to elucidate the puzzling detail of removing her bra, emerged as I read the studies of dreaming in color by Freud and Richard V. Yazmajian. Their reports of case histories not only reinforced my initial surmise but greatly enriched its implications for the understanding of *Il deserto rosso*. With their help, I propose that an antithesis of menstruation and masturbation that previously eluded my analysis may play a decisive role in this episode.

In his own synopsis of his article "Color in Dreams", Yazmajian wrote:

Color and color contrasts are utilized by the ego to give disguised representation to childhood memory traces of the color contrasts perceived on viewing genitals and pubic hair of adults and children. Mechanisms used by the ego to effect this are described and compared to those observed in the case of screen memories, fetishism, and the day residue. The same psychodynamics and mechanisms are shown to be present in cases where color assumes a role in a fantasy, in a symptom, and in sublimation.

The film tells us nothing of Giuliana's childhood. If the story she tells her son may be said to reflect her screen memory of that childhood, it would be all we have to go on. Even so, her 'confession' of the young girl's antipathy to adults and other children suggests the appropriateness of Yazmajian's analogy, even if nothing in the film can ever confirm evidence of an exposure to genitals.

There are uncanny coincidences in his summary of 'Case History A' in his "Dreams Completely in Color" and aspects of the film; for the leading actress, Monica Vitti, who was the filmmaker's long-term partner at the time and the star of two of the three previous films, was a blonde who dyed her hair red for *Il deserto rosso*. She portrays Giuliana as a frigid woman, overwhelmed by phobias. (Antonioni has said that she felt much closer to the character of Giuliana than to that of Vittoria, the role she had in his previous film, *Eclisse*. [1962])

Her projection of an imaginary case of polio on her son, Fabrizio, was the proximate occasion for the 'memory' seen in extra-vivid color. Yazmajian again:

> Prominent among the neurotic symptoms which led a twenty-eight-year-old unmarried woman to seek analysis were frigidity and multiple phobias... Dreams were rather infrequently recalled, but color elements were present in the large majority of those which she did remember. A dream was reported in the session preceding the one in which she described a totally colored dream. This dream, which is pertinent to the understanding of the dream to be considered, consisted of observing herself in a mirror and noting that her hair was reddish-blond in color. She then streaked her hair with a black crayon. The patient is blond; her mother is a red-head; the father's hair is black. The dream occurred on the last day of her menstrual period. Each of these facts was given representation in the color elements. Other determinants of the dream were masturbatory primal scene conflicts and her fearful wish about identifying with her "castrated" mother. The most central aspect of the session was the further working through of typical vaginal displacement and fetishistic mechanisms. This too was represented in the dream by displacement and a fetishistic use of color and color contrasts...Her distortions of reality also reemerged in this context.

Freud himself had offered a case history relevant to Yazmajian's in "A Tentative Psychological Theory of Acquired Hysteria, Many Phobias and Obsessions, and Certain Hallucinatory Psychoses" (1912). Coincidentally, there is a striking similarity of the effect of reading a magazine on both Freud's patient and Giuliana, who imagined Fabrizio had polio after reading of the disease at his bedside:

> A young girl suffers from obsessive reproaches. If she reads anything in the journal about false coiners, she conceives the thought that she too, made counterfeit money; if a murder was anywhere committed by an unknown assassin, she anxiously asked herself whether she had not committed this crime. At the same time, she is perfectly aware of the absurdity of these obsessive reproaches. For a time, the consciousness of her guilt gained such a power over her that her judgment was suppressed, and she accused herself before her relatives and physician of having really committed all these crimes (Psychosis through simple aggravation – overwhelming psychosis). A thorough examination revealed the source of the origin of this guilty conscience. Accidentally incited by a sensual feeling, she allowed herself to be allured by a friend to masturbate. She practiced it for years with the full consciousness of her wrongdoing, and under the most violent but useless self-reproaches.

These case histories can help us to spell out what is latent in the *ambivalent* iconography of the episode. I stress *ambivalent* because of the antithetical nature of such icons: the girl is both a figure of the virgin Diana surrounded by wild creatures *and* an emblem of Venus with her libidinous rabbit; the white Narcissus flower she sniffs is the traditional religious image of the purity of Paradise and of the blessed Virgin Mary *and* a clue to her autoerotic narcissism; when she gratuitously uncovers her chest she is invoking the romantic ship to come or her, from which she both hides in the shrubbery *and* swims out to meet; *and*, extrapolating from the psychoanalytic interpretations recorded here, I propose that by removing the top of her bathing suit, she is displacing the shedding of the lower piece to repress the recollection of masturbation and/or menstruation. The fusions of fear and pleasurable excitement, of menstruation and masturbation generate the psychotic ambivalences that control the style of the film and the erratic behavior of its protagonist. The unacknowledged detail of removing the bra in the heavily stressed mystery of the landscape is a visual provocation, a clue, to the psychological – even psychoanalytical – mystery of the film's subject.

Philosophers of the cinema who were born before 1950 experienced the transition from almost totally black and white films to an even greater ubiquity of those in color. Thus, they often speculated on the qualities of the best color films, as if they shared a unique inflection. Stanley Cavell noted:

> I have recorded my experience of the work of color in series films as a de-psychologizing or un-theatricalizing of their subjects. My hypo--thesis is that, correctly understood, this would account for the feel of futurity in them (when, that is, the point is not the colorization of make-believe or the color symbolism of private fantasy).

He specifically alluded to Antonioni's first color film as an example of futurity, when he wrote: "Among the works of serious directors, *Red Desert* is almost as explicit as the unfortunate *Fahrenheit 451* in its premonition that the world we live in is already the world of the future." [p82]. But he would have been justified in seeing the episode of the girl on the beach – in a *different* register of color within the color film – as an example of "private fantasy." Nothing in *Marnie* passes for "private fantasy." The aesthetic problem of Marnie's reactions to the color red might be Hitchcock's refusal to grant her privacy of any sort. Antonioni's emphasis on "private fantasy" is the measure of his refusal of finding a simple cause, violent or not, for Giuliana's neurosis.

Persona
and
Zerkalo [The Mirror]

I came out of retirement in July 2023 to accept an offer from the Cinemateca portuguesa to give five lectures. I was uncertain whether I wanted to show Ingmar Bergman's *Persona* (1966) or Andrei Tarkovsky's *Zerkalo* [*The Mirror*, 1975] as an example of a Primal Scene drama. Fortunately, *Persona* was not available, making the choice simple. I write "fortunately" because when I opted to show excerpts from *Persona* during the final lecture, centered on *Zerkalo*, I noted an even more intimate connection between the two films than I had previously realized. That connection generated this book. I hasten to add that I believe the relationship was unconscious on Tarkovsky's part, for the initial viewing of both films suggests few affinities. That may have been because in *Zerkalo* the zoom lens and zooming does a good deal of the work traditionally assigned to cutting: that is typical of Tarkovsky's other films and of Bergman's films made in the 70s and 80s.

Aside from the two pre-title sequences involving adolescent boys and cinematic (or television) apparatuses, the coincidences between the two films are far from obvious. At times my comparison seems like a far-fetched checklist. Whereas *Persona* is a concise, but mysterious drama occurring between two women over a short time, *Zerkalo* is a diffuse scattering of memories, newsreels, urban myths, dreams and family stories spanning nearly half a century. The contrast between the pessimistic psychologist Bergman and the mystical metaphysician Tarkovsky is radical and an impediment to comparison. One gets the impression that even later, in his Italian and Swedish films, when he used Bergman's actors in his own films, Tarkovsky was insisting, "No. I am not Ingmar Bergman; I am Andrei Tarkovsky!" (to paraphrase the climax of *Persona*); his films mean and look unmistakably different. In noticing and studying the syntax of Bergman's art, he discovered what cinema could do – *his* cinema; and he ran with it.

My interpretation of *Persona* in *Modernist Montage* (1990) depended upon the rarity and strategic uses of shot-countershot to establish an allegory of psychoanalysis (while maintaining that the filmmaker was essentially hostile to the process). I didn't realize until I saw the film again in Lisbon, that shot-countershot is even rarer in *Zerkalo* than in *Persona*. It has only one extended shot-countershot exchange: between Maria and Lisa in the printshop in 1935. Like the climactic exchange in *Persona*, it is the occasion for Lisa to attack the personality of Maria in a most cutting manner, by calling upon events she could not possibly have witnessed. There is but one other instance of genuine shot-countershot in *Zerkalo*: when a boy (who appears only once in the film) talks to the drillmaster; it is not a sustained exchange but merely one shot matching another. There are several false shot-countershot matches: most dramatically when, late in the film, after Maria tries to sell her earrings to the doctor's wife, soon after chopping the head off a rooster, she looks off, in color, and her glance is matched by a black and white shot of her husband, just before she levitates. Earlier, similarly the redhaired girl with a cold-sore seems to look once to the drillmaster in a parallel false exchange. Later, Alexei seems to be looking at the doctor's wife as she jabbers on. I write "seems" because these examples are both fleeting and ambiguous.

A comparison of the script for *Persona* with the finished film revealed that Bergman constructed what I take to be the allegory of psychoanalysis while editing the film. Most of the points that are crucial to my interpretation were not in the initial shooting script. Likewise, it is known that Tarkovsky edited several radically different versions of *Zerkalo* before deciding on the shape of the completed work. Its overall structure remains tentative, and appears to be arbitrary, while *Persona*'s mysteries seem intentional and well-planned. Nevertheless, Bergman may have been the filmmaker Tarkovsky most admired. I suspect that the model of *Persona* underwrote *Zerkalo*'s unusual mode of construction, that would have been more typical of the making of many short avant-garde films. Yet I do not believe the relation of *Zerkalo* to *Persona* was deliberate, or even conscious.

Several times in *Zerkalo*'s opening sequence of Maria sitting on the dacha fence, she seems to be in a shot exchange with the doctor who flirts with her, but the zooming and reframing of the moving camera undermines that logic. Once the camera cuts explicitly from her turned face to her two sleeping children in a hammock (as unexpected as the old man sleeping in *Les vacances de M.Hulot* while Hulot waits for his date), but the exchanges with the doctor do not fit normal shot-countershot patterns. In fact, because shot-countershot is rarer in *Zerkalo* than in *Persona*; and because frequently it is obviously false, it hardly calls attention to itself as a systematic signpost. The latter's false matches include the Spanish girl with a doll, in the touching newsreel sequence of the Spanish Communists' children evacuated to Russia; she gives a disturbed stare that cuts to Chkalov and his stratospheric balloon; similarly, once the editing makes the redhaired girl in *Zerkalo* look to a naked soldier in the Sivash newsreel; finally, Tarkovsky cuts from Maria looking out of the shed with potatoes in black and white to a farmhouse landscape in color.

The equivalent of *Zerkalo*'s newsreels would be the documents of two historical events that intrude on *Persona*. Both are psychological indices: rather than signposts for dating other materials: Elisabet looks at the photograph of a boy in the Warsaw ghetto and at the televised self-immolation of a Vietnamese monk. Both characteristically represent history as a horror-story, while Tarkovsky's newsreels mix disasters with nationalist achievements, protests with celebrations, the black and white past of the movie experience with the present, vivid black and white inserts into a world in color. The borderline zones of barely recalled dreams and dubious family tales in the film share that black and white domain.

Tarkovsky apparently identified with the boys, Ignat and the defiant orphan of the Leningrad blockade. He even had to be persuaded *not* to show his own face in the deathbed scene when he releases the bird that landed on the defiant boy's head in the imitation of Brueghel's 'Winter' (aka 'The Return of the Hunters'). Both two scenes with the bird are much too contrived to be convincing.

Ignat, like Moses in Exodus, stands before a fire as his parents argue about his fate; there is also an allusion to Moses in the pretitle sequence; for the Hebrew prophet too had to overcome his tongue-tied speech to lead his people from slavery. By implication, Tarkovsky overcame fiscal and bureaucratic impediments in order to make this film and, in fact, earn his poet-father's admiration in making it.

The filmmaker attached three of his father's poems, written much later, to scenes ostensibly from the 1930s, and one to a WWII scene. The anachronistic and misplaced origins of Arsenyi Tarkovsky's poems, written after his divorce to the filmmaker's mother, and sometimes for other women, represent the boy's latent desire to reunite his parents. There is almost no indication of Arsenyi Tarkovsky's other wives, unless Tarkovsky's casting of his own *second* wife as the doctor's wife would be a displacement of it. However, there is one occasion when Alexei, offscreen, tells Natalya he wants Ignat to live with him and *his* "second wife."

According to the distinguished psychoanalyst, Jacob Arlow, fire plays a central role in the revenge motives in Primal Scene fantasies. Fire is part of the Primal Scene episode in *Zerkalo* where the ceiling caves in; it also accompanies most of the memories of the redhaired girl; it dominates in the burning shed; it even appears right after the printing house episode; and last of all, in the dacha of the doctor's wife. In several of these cases it is linked to excessive water.

In *Modernist Montage* I made extensive use of Henry Edelheit's *primal scene schema* to establish the allegory of psychoanalysis in *Persona*. His five questions initially struck me as closely reflecting my experience of the film. However, I did not think that *Zerkalo* fit that schema when I *wrote* about it in *The Cinema of Poetry* (2015). There I was wrong. In Lisbon I realized that they applied to *Zerkalo* as well, if not so blatantly. Here are Edelheit's five questions raised by primal scene experiences:

> 1} What *is* happening? 2) To whom is it happening? Who is the victim and who the aggressor? 3) How many people are involved? One? Two? Several? Or is it one composite creature? 4) What *is* the anatomy of the scene? If it is made up of more than one individual, which one has the penis? 5) Where am I (the observer)? Am I participating or am I excluded?

Initially I had not recalled that in addition to the image of crucifixion, Edelheit had given equal significance to the association with bullfights as characteristic clues of a primal scene disturbance. One bullfight introduces the newsreel from the Spanish Civil War. In fact, one of the few false countershot's shows Maria and Ignat (or Alexei) staring at their Spanish refugee housemate reenacting Palamo Linares' role of matador. The newsreels that follow it in rapid succession provide "historical" keys to affixing dates to the scattered memories in the film.

The construction of *Zerkalo* is so complex that "What is happening?" would be an appropriate question, but 2) and 3) are most convincing. Although Tarkovsky did not split the screen to fuse nurse and patient as Bergman did, instead he cast the same actors as Alexei's *wife and mother*, and the *same boy* to play the adolescent *sons, Ignat and Alexei;* he used his natural mother as the mother of Alexei and his second wife as the nasty wife of the doctor to whom Maria attempted to sell her earrings to have food. Such casting endows the film with a powerful Oedipal charge. Likewise, in a paramount instance of Oedipal revenge, Andrei Tarkovsky bestowed international prestige upon by father's poems just by including his voice and poems in the film.

At times Maria seems the *victim* of Lisa, Alexei, and of the doctor's wife. At times she is the *victimizer* of Ignat or Alexei. The daughter of the Spaniard imitating Linares is also a victim of her father's sudden rage, perhaps at her sexual maturity, but claiming that he is angry because she dared to do a Gypsy dance after years of denying her Spanish heritage, as if she were a native Russian. Other victims include the bull, the fake body of dead Hitler, the photographic image of the soldier with one leg (the wartime affliction of Arsenyi Tarkovsky), the Spanish refugees and their grieved relatives, and the rooster Maria has to kill.

The fifth question makes the correspondences far-fetched: it is far from as clear as in the case of *Persona*, unless one considers the act of reconstructing the false countershots as an ambiguous index of participation. As for who has the penis: like Bergman's weak or "blind" men, in *Zerkalo* the one potent man is the absent father. The only sex Maria has is with Ignat's father, despite his taunts to her after their divorce about her wannabe author as a lover; earlier that father had impertinently asked about his son's girlfriends. The redhaired girl enters the film as his father's confessed or boasting memory of her erotic attraction, associated in his son's mind with fire and the imagery of Georges de la Tour.

The broken fence and the creaking sound of the cradle-like hammock introduce the Primal Scene that is reflected at the end of the film when the protagonist's death immediately precedes the father and mother in a field talking of the potential gender of the child they have (presumably) just conceived. Soon after the opening "screen-memory," of the fence and hammock, the boy awakes to wind in trees, calling "Papa" as his father washes his mother's hair. Then the ceiling falls, as if his early primal memory or fantasy turned violently apocalyptic. Later, in the earring scene the boy, now much older, calls "Mama." Here the violence is displaced to the beheading of a rooster. Previously, a rooster broke through a glass pane, in a scene of displaced deflowering.

What Pasolini calls "free indirect subjective" abounds: the adolescents in the pre-title scenes of both *Persona* and *Zerkalo* were the subjects of cinematic creativity. But for Bergman the pivot is a parody of an early one-reel comedy of primal scene images, while Tarkovsky invokes an Apollonian wind as a "spiritual source" of inspiration.

Later, the camera movement displaces the function of the wind as it probes Maria's apartment during Alexei's telephone call. In a parallel scene, Alexei's long criticism of his ex-wife, Natalya, and their son, Ignat, occurs in a similar (or the same) apartment with his voice always offscreen. Natalya looks at herself in several mirrors while Alexei accuses her of making a poor choice of lover and of failing as a mother. It is a demonstration of erotic jealousy, reflecting the one displaced in *Persona* when Alma has sex with Elisabet's husband in front of her, and behind her back, literally.

In *Persona*, the erotic attraction of Alma for Elisabet is signaled by a mirror image. In *Zerkalo*, other prominent mirrors occur as when a Spanish woman runs for cover with a broken mirror; the doctor's wife keeps checking how the earrings look on her in mirrors. Exceptionally, young Alexei looks into a mirror as he waits in the doctor's house while his mother tries to sell the earrings. There, the zoom into the mirror image reverses to a zoom into the boy's face, and cuts to a specular image of the redhaired girl before a fire, hinting that his father spied on her with the drillmaster. When he turns his head, we see a flickering gas-lamp as if from his viewpoint. At the invitation of the doctor's wife, he looks at her sleeping baby son. When Maria looks toward the crib, the baby opens his eyes in countershot. The sight of the baby seems to make her ill, as if she desired to kill it rather than the rooster.

The recurring images of wind, indoors and out, indicate, as I stated, poetic inspiration. When Ignat stands before a fire, like Moses, his mother (echoing the filmmaker's often explicit sexism) complains that no gift of prophecy ever came to her. (Tarkovsky claimed women are meant to sacrifice themselves for their children). In the very end, when the boy walks in the fields with the grandmother and his sister, three bird calls answer his elaborate hooting. In this post-mortem fantasy, he has entered totally into the natural world, abetted by Baroque choral music. There is no place for such a "religious" conclusion in Bergman's cinema, although the final "psychological" vision of Isaak's parents at the end of *Wild Strawberries* may have influenced Tarkovsky's transcendental epilogue, as I suggested in *The Cinema of Poetry*. Bergman's world is permeated by misanthropy; his hatred of his father was unremitted. (Nearly all the fathers in Bergman's films are despicable.) Tarkovsky, on the other hand, idealized the parent-child relationship and he believed in the redemptive power of art, connecting poets of all sorts to powers beyond their comprehension. For him the Primal Scene is not the nagging demon it is for Bergman, but the "prophetic" source of great art, that of Leonardo, Bach, Breughel (and Bergman).

Marnie (1964).

Red Desert (1964).

Mirror (1974).

Persona (1966).

O Thiassos [The Travelliing Players]
and
Xi meng ren sheng [The Puppetmaster]

Two veteran filmmakers, Theo Angelopoulos and Hou Hsiao Hsien, separated by half the globe, in Greece and in Taiwan, incorporated into their masterpieces reflections of the troubled histories of their nations: *O Tiassos*, [*The Troup*, called *The Travelling Players* in the USA] (1975) and *Xi meng ren sheng*, [literally *Drama, Dream, Life* called *The Puppetmaster* in the USA] (1993).

Similarly, in the twilight of celluloid cinema several film-makers, in addition to Angelopoulos and Hou, have introduced nations new to the medium (or with renewed force, as in India and Russia) with their major works: from Portugal, New Zealand, Hungary, and Lithuania, i.e. Mani Kaul, *Siddheshwari* (1978), Manoel Oliviera, *Amor de Perdição* [*Doomed Love*] (1979), Jane Campion, *Angel at My Table* (1990) Bela Tarr, *Satantango* (1993), Sharunas Bartas, *Koridorius*, [*The Corridor*] (1995), and Alexander Sokurov, *Russkij kovcheg* [*Russian Ark*] (2002).

O Thiasos alludes to the history of Greece from 1939 to 1952, from the end of the Metaxas dictatorship, through the Italian war, WWII and the Nazi occupation of Greece, and the postwar civil strife between Communists and Anglo-American forces. As the actors travel from one provincial town to another, performing the naïve rustic drama, *Golfo the Shepherdess*, the film moves between the present and several time zones in the past. The model for the plot is obviously Aeschylus' *Oresteia*. In updating it, Angelopoulos posited Clytemnestra and her lover Aegisthos as Nazi sympathizers and betrayers of her cuckolded husband, Agamemnon, whom the Nazi execute as a member of the Resistance. Their leftist son, Orestes kills the informing couple. Instead of being pursued by the Erinyes, the rightwing authorities arrest and shoot him. One of his sisters, Electra carries on his cause while another, Chrysothemis, becomes a collaborating prostitute, a British ally and an American wife (in the *Oresteia*, her father had sacrificed her for a safe voyage to Troy). Pylades, Orestes' close friend, marries Electra before he is captured, tortured, and opts for rightwing survival. As soon as the military junta of the Greek colonels collapsed, the film was released to great success.

Stan Brakhage, speaking about Andrei Tarkovsky at the Telluride Film Festival where *Nostaghia* (1983) was shown, said:

> The three greatest tasks for film in the 20th Century are 1) to make the epic, that is, to tell the tales of the tribes of the world. 2) to keep it personal, because only in the eccentricities of our personal lives do we have any chance at the truth. 3) To do the dream work, that is, to illuminate the borders of the unconscious.

Probably unknown to Brakhage, the films of Angelopoulos and Hou do precisely all three tasks.

Hou's actual title for the film suggests the sentence 'Life is a Dream on Stage'. The filmmaker's personal identification with the aged puppetmaster, Li Tianlu, is obvious and well documented. James Udden refers to him as a substitute father. The film is actually a fusion of a documentary bio-pic and an oneiric 'history' of Taiwan between 1911 and 1945. Li himself pops up occasionally in the film, telling his life story to the camera. More often his voice narrates offscreen. But Hou plays very freely with the temporality of his narratives. Udden gives a fine description of one of these strange depictions:

> ...the subtle strains of Chen Mingzhan's guitar music chimes in as
> well, only to slowly segue into the next scene where the children are
> introduced to the stepmother. Certainly such sonic layering in itself is
> not that unusual and can be found in Hollywood films. What is
> unusual is that in this case one can hardly pick out the actual
> narrative ellipsis due to the continuous sound, nor the temporal
> disruption at work in this last image: the script makes very clear that
> those carriages, which appear on the screen before Li even gets to
> talking about his mother's actual death, are actually transporting his
> new stepmother to their house. Thus, while we hear from Li an
> accounting of an event already past and never seen, the visuals on
> screen are already well into the future since the carriages indicate
> that Li's father has already remarried. Sound here not only lets past
> and future flow into each other without any clear borderlines, it hides
> its stratagems under a guise of spontaneity and unforced naturalism,
> the hallmarks of the film's creator.

Sometimes it takes a viewer of *O Thiassos* a few seconds to
decipher the clues of the time period of a new episode, but it is
never as indecipherable and intricate as this. For instance, some
two hours into the film, we see Li in a rural setting as his children
set off firecrackerss. There is an empty coffin in the foreground of
the shot. In the following shot, we hear hammering and the
crying of his grandchild. Li takes a drink, lights his pipe, and
tells his daughter that he slept in the empty coffin. A fourth shot
reveals that he is sick, as his wife and daughter minister to him.
Eventually the voiceover tells us that his father and young son
have died of malaria in the coffin shop to which he was assigned
in the evacuation of Taipei (ironically on the day the war ended).
The complex interweaving of the end of the war (the cause of the
firecrackers), malaria, two deaths in the family, a useless move
from Taipei, and the coffin shop are all otherwise unexplained
matters until the delayed narration clarifies them.

Both *O Thiassos* and Xi *meng ren sheng* are made up of very
long-held sequence-shots; in the latter the camera seldom budges.
They depict historical circumstances over decades from the point-

of-view of individuals living and working far from the centers of power. Both are what Brakhage called "Tales of the Tribe." Hou's history of Taiwan emerged from his search for an authentic Chinese art form, and amalgam of Confucian, Taoist, and Buddhist elements.

Influenced by the Peking opera, Chinese narratives, and traditional landscape painting, it employs no shot-countershot, seldom using more than one shot per episode in its complex inter-weaving of voiceover autobiography and imagery that occasion-ally leaps into the present of Li's narrative. In its search for an authentic, non-western cinema it tells the history of the Japanese occupation of Taiwan from the point of view of a "living national treasure," whose magical thinking suggests the puppet theater as protocinema, virtually lost in late 20th century.

Alexandr Sukorov achieved the fantasy of Alfred Hitchcock's *Rope* (1948) of making a feature-length film in one shot. *Russkij kovcheg* was recorded in uncompressed high-definition video using a Sony HDW-F900 SteadyCam. It took four tries to make the 90-minute film without a break, and it required elaborate post-production refinements. In it the contemptuous homosexual, Astolphe de Custine (1790-1857), who visited and wrote about Russia in 1838, accompanies an anonymous narrator through the Winter Palace in St. Petersburg as a tour of modern Russian and Soviet history until the entire Hermitage and the massive gathering of aristocracy within it floats through the Neva River into Eternity, as if it were an "ark.". Every room the camera entered and passes through represents another phase of that history, as we encounter Peter the Great, Catherine the Great, Czars Nicolas 1 and 2, and the siege of Leningrad by the Nazis. The final scene is an extravagant ball set in 1913 with a cast of thousands.

More indirectly *Koridorius* refracts the history of modern Lithuania, while *Siddheshwari*, *An Angel at My Table*, and *Satantango* present modern India, New Zealand, and Hungary through the lives of a singer, a writer, and failed terrorists. All these films recognize the power of cinema to personalize national histories.

Morgan Fisher
and
Hollis Frampton

The comparison of the entire limited filmography of Morgan Fisher with some films from the more extensive one of Hollis Frampton would be the least "incongruent" pairing in this book. They are, or were, remarkably similar filmmakers.

In a ten-minute video clip of a lecture Morgan Fisher gave at the European Graduate School in Switzerland in 2007, he presented himself with characteristically understated bravado as a rebel, if not a heretic, among avant-garde filmmakers:

> In the world in which I began, synch (sound) was regarded with suspicion, and the privileged mode was the silent film; not only that, but there was a privileged piece of apparatus – there was a camera that was the politically correct kind of camera to have. That camera was the Bolex... and if you had a Bolex it was already a kind of credential. I never owned a Bolex; so, I was suspect. Not only that, I made films not just with sound, but with synch sound... Not only that but it attached itself to the industry, through its terms... Movies always wanted movies to be synch; they were synch in principle...

In the fall of 2005 the Whitney Museum of American Art in New York mounted three remarkable retrospectives of avant-garde filmmakers of the same artistic generation: All three – Robert Beavers, Owen Land (born George Landow), and Morgan

Fisher – began making films that attracted attention in the Sixties, and all three were still quite young when they began to show their films, (Beavers and Landow were teenagers when they screened their first films; Fisher was in his mid-twenties). That October, the Whitney's Assistant Curator of Film and Video, Henriette Huldisch, brought together the most comprehensive program of Beavers's films ever shown. The Landow program, organized by independent curator Mark Webber for LUX in London, came to the Whitney in November, after traveling extensively in Europe, Australia, and the US. Lastly, the museum programmed (following its debut at Tate Modern, London) "Standard Gauge: Film Works by Morgan Fisher, 1968–2003," organized by the Whitney's chief curator of film and video, Chrissie Iles. An advocate for the incorporation of film pieces in gallery spaces, Iles included one of Fisher's installations to complement this nine-film retrospective.

Together these three retrospectives reminded us of the vigor with which young artists empowered themselves as filmmakers in the '60s. The exuberance, self-confidence, even cockiness of the earliest films in these exhibitions reveal the aesthetic optimism of fledgling American filmmakers nearly eighty years ago. Yet even within the narrow span of their moments of entry there were significant gradations in how their initial films were greeted and in how the filmmakers subsequently progressed. In 1964, Jonas Mekas showed Landow's first 16mm film, the silent *Fleming Faloon* (1963–64), at the Film-Makers' Cinematheque and then included it in the International Exhibition of the New American Cinema traveling through Europe. By 1967 Landow had released two more silent 16mm films and, in 1968 and 1969, two more with sound, firmly establishing his reputation as one of the most promising young avant-garde filmmakers and winning him a full-time teaching position at the School of the Art Institute of Chicago. (He made almost all of his films as George Landow, not changing his name to Land until the early '80s, when he was no longer active as a filmmaker.) At seventeen, Robert Beavers completed *Spiracle* (1966), which he showed two years later at the Experimental Film Competition in Knokke-le-Zoute, Belgium. By then he had moved to Europe, where he has lived and worked ever since, seldom showing his films in public, except when European cinémathèques purchased prints of them. Devoted enthusiasts of his work had to make their way to the Temenos screenings held in central Greece nearly every summer in the 1980s to count on seeing just one of his films. In the late '90s he began to present some of his work in America, but the Whitney retrospective was the first occasion for it to be seen *en masse*.

Fisher is two years older than Landow and seven years older than Beavers, but he was the last to start his career. Two early films: *The Director and His Actor Look at Footage Showing Preparations for an Unmade Film* (1968) and *Phi Phenomenon* (1968), attracted attention the year they were made, at the film festivals of Hunter College (New York City) and the Maryland College of Art (Baltimore). Within six years Fisher had completed another eight films. The early '70s was a period of intense cinematic productivity for Fisher's strongest peers; in that company, his films earned him a respectable but modest reputation. A transitional work, *Projection Instructions* (1976), called for the intervention of a projectionist (following printed instructions) in the screening of an otherwise conventionally exhibited film. Subsequently, Fisher turned his attention to film installations twenty years before museums and galleries would embrace such work, making and exhibiting *Southern Exposure* (1977), *North Light* (1979), *Passing Time* (1979), and *Color Balance* (1980).

Returning to filmmaking in 1984, he completed his longest film (thirty-five minutes) and most impressive film, *Standard Gauge* (1984). Then, after an extraordinary pause of nineteen years, he followed it with *()* (2003), a brilliant twenty-one-minute film, sometimes informally called "Parenthesis."

When Landow and Beavers were making their first films, Fisher was at school; first at Harvard, where he majored in art history (1960–64), then the film school of the University of

Southern California (1964–65), and, finally, the film school at UCLA (1965–66). Landow and Beavers were autodidacts, shaped by the avant-garde films they saw in their teens; they may have been the last of many masters of the American avant-garde cinema who either avoided college or dropped out: Kenneth Anger, Stan Brakhage, Marie Menken, Larry Jordan, Harry Smith, Jack Smith, Ken Jacobs, Gregory Markopoulos, Hollis Frampton, Jerome Hiler, and Jonas Mekas.

Fisher's formal education and his decision, after 1970, to remain working in the film industry in Los Angeles profoundly affected the character of his art. He seems to have moved into avant-garde cinema as a consequence of his "disaffection "with the limitations of conventional narratives; very quickly he became the most academically reductive practitioner of the minimalist filmmaking I delineated at the time as "structural film" (in an essay in *Film Culture* [Summer 1969] that would turn out to be the most controversial of my career as a critic). Yet, "structural film" was largely a New York (and London) phenomenon, molded and enlivened by the friendships and rivalries of like-minded filmmakers. In Southern California, Fisher was radically isolated (along with his friend, Thom Anderson) and, perhaps for that reason, fascinated by the theory and criticism of the visual arts.

For most of the other North American makers of "structural" films, long duration and repetitive, minimalized imagery were means to achieve versions of the sublime. Fisher, however, steadfastly resisted the sublime. Instead, he invented cinematic paradoxes, pitting montage against very long takes. In the academy these would have been seen as the opposition to the film theories of Sergei Eisenstein and André Bazin, but in avant-garde practice an antinomy of the extreme long takes of Andy Warhol with the montage practice of Peter Kubelka and Bruce Conner were closer to his sights. He seems to have been an avid reader of *Film Culture*, *Artforum*, and later *October*; in his occasional writings on his films, he cites Michael Fried and Rosalind Krauss – both of whom overlapped his years at Harvard – as well as Yve-

Alain Bois and Benjamin Buchloh, who taught at Harvard long after he graduated. Fisher's relative isolation and intellectual intensity contributed to the rigorous and hermetic, almost agoraphobic, character of his early films. Apart from the very first one he made, they were all shot indoors, in stripped-down studios, in which the dominant human presence, when there is one, is the filmmaker himself. George Landow, who once used him in a film, described his screen persona as a Milquetoast professor-poet. That earnest, somewhat timid demeanor stages his deadpan wit, often making his ironic "explanations" for the camera operations very funny.

The process of filmmaking, its tools, and its jargon have been Fisher's subject for at least fifty years. Reseeing his first film from the perspective of the Whitney retrospective, we can find all of his central strategies in place from the very start. *The Director and His Actor...* is a film in two parts. In the first, we see a barren room with a young man sitting behind a tape recorder. Another man, played by Fisher himself, busily enters and leaves the room; he tests the recording machine and eventually goes into a back room, which, when illuminated, turns out to be a projection booth. The film he projects will be the whole second part of this work. It, in turn, is divided into six parts. Through all of them we hear the offhand comments of the two young men as they watch the rushes of their film. In principle, the film they watch is a single long take of a screen on which many shorter shots are projected: First, there are sixty-one very short shots, presumably edited in camera, of the two men taking still photographs of a residential neighborhood, empty lots, and of each other; then, from a single camera setup, in a sequence of eighteen jump-cuts, we see Fisher develop the rolls of 35mm still film and, in three more, hanging them to dry in another corner of the darkroom. Next, there is a long take from behind of Fisher meticulously laying out a title card and twenty photographs corresponding to images we saw him shooting earlier, followed by the silent film he made of them. Finally, his actor repeats the process; first, he messily assembles his twenty photographs at the same table, from the same angle; then we see his film of stills, which includes images of Fisher shooting him and of the two previously unacknowledged crew members who filmed both the director and his actor.

The two films-within-the-film-in-progress-within-the-film are closer in spirit to Chris Marker's science-fiction masterpiece in stills, *La Jetée* (1962), and Agnès Varda's documentary *Salut les cubains* (1963) than to the later, aggressive structural films made with stills by Michael Snow (*One Second in Montreal* [1969]) and Hollis Frampton (*Hapax Legomena: (nostalgia)*). Poised between dramatic and apodictic forms immanent in his initial effort, Fisher quickly opted for the latter. His *Phi Phenomenon* (1968) stares at a wall clock without a second hand. The title refers to the illusion of movement generated by the rapid substitution of proximate images, say, two lights on a marquee. It is central to all cinematic perception, but Fisher makes us sweat out eleven minutes vainly trying to catch the minute hand in motion. His minimalism would never again be so niggardly. That same year he filmed a naked woman with a tape recorder (*Documentary Footage*), first asking a series of questions about her body, then answering them. If the ascetic *Phi Phenomenon* atones for the prurient wit of *Documentary Footage*, more significantly, it initiates the depletion of connotation typical of his rejection of the sublime in his subsequent films of the '70s. Fisher tempers this ascesis with an obsessive fondness for the film equipment he photographs.

Production Stills (1970), a refinement of the employment of still photographs, is a perfectly enclosed narrative of its own production: The image is one long take of a wall on which a hand sequentially pins a number of Polaroids, one after the other, again for eleven minutes (the running time of a four-hundred-foot roll of 16mm film). The Polaroids depict the crew making the film; the synchronous sound allows us to hear without interruption in "real time" their chatter and the hum of the static camera, so that we can anticipate the photos and assign faces to the voices we hear. In a similar vein, *Picture and Sound Rushes* (1973) and *Cue Rolls*

(1974) explore respectively the parameters of synchronous sound and 'a- and b-roll editing' as ironically didactic demonstrations. The tension between a very long take and montage operates in different registers in each of these films. Yet its most elaborate form occurs in *Standard Gauge*, which is an uninterrupted tour-de-force performance for thirty-two minutes, the maximum length of a 16mm shot. Warhol had utilized this duration repeatedly in the mid-'60s for nearly static subjects, but Fisher composed his long take of a series of nearly thirty strips of film unwound with individual frames repeatedly held for scrutiny under the unblinking gaze of his camera.

Turning his formidable self-deprecating irony on his obsessions, Fisher commented offscreen on this collection of 35mm (which is to say, 'standard gauge') film snippets he assembled over years. In so doing he tangentially elaborated his anti-sublime theory of the beauty of cinematic ephemera and articulated his autobiography as a filmmaker, as Hollis Frampton had done to an opposite effect showing and talking about his still photographs in *Hapax Legomena: (nostalgia)*. Whereas Frampton crammed his film with images and stories about the art-world celebrities with whom he worked (Andre, Stella, Rosenquist, Poons, Snow), Fisher stresses the marginal situation of his friends and himself – making ends meet by editing low budget films, subtitling, researching stock footage, and playing bit roles that ended up on the cutting-room floor. Whereas Frampton talked himself into a drama of an unexplained uncanny event that made him give up still photography, Fisher lets his film peter out with, as he puts it, "some pieces of film that I think are interesting to look at." For him the somewhat uncanny moment came earlier, when a lab technician handed him a decomposing clip of camera original from a newsreel Bruce Conner had used prominently in *A Movie* (1958), the most influential film in the genre of *Standard Gauge*.

Yet Frampton's sensibility, not Conner's, would be the closest to Fisher's among the major American avant-garde filmmakers.

They both present themselves as intellectually sophisticated, severe ironists, meticulous craftsmen, and philosophically inclined didactic professionals meting out insider information. Of the two, Frampton was by far the more prolific and expansive artist – and the more caustic satirist. They began to exhibit films at the same moment: Frampton's breakthrough film, *Surface Tension* (1968), drew attention and prizes at the same two festivals where I, and many others, first saw Fisher's work. But Frampton quickly won a degree of critical recognition that came to Fisher only after he released *Standard Gauge*. Film historians Scott MacDonald and Paul Arthur have written well on Fisher, and he is one of the heroes of David E. James's splendid book, *The Most Typical Avant-Garde: History and Geography of Minor Cinemas in Los Angeles* (University of California Press, 2005).

Fisher's most recent film, (), succeeds astonishingly where Frampton's parallel effort, *Hapax Legomena: Remote Control* (1972) failed; it uses aleatory methods to release the narrative unconscious of a set of randomly selected films. () is made up entirely of "inserts" from feature films organized on covert Oulipian principles. Inserts were usually shot by assistants when star actors, large crews, or expensive sets were not needed. They include details of weapons, wounds, letters, signs, tombstones, machinery, games of chance, time pieces, money, and even intimate caresses. Fisher culled the inserts from a number of films he collected for that purpose and edited them together under constraints he does not fully reveal; he places the inserts from a given film in the order in which they appeared in that film, but two inserts from the same film never follow each other directly in his assemblage. Alternating among them we catch glimpses of violence, intrigue, high-stakes gambling, and sexual adventure.

Fisher has not been utterly solitary in his isolation. He credits his longtime friend and sometimes collaborator, Thom Anderson, with the inspiration for (). In 1966–67 Andersen edited --- ------- (often called "Short Line, Long Line" or "the rock 'n' roll film"), a montage of rock-music images in which each pair of shots contains a short shot followed by a longer one; the first shot of the following pair is longer than the short one of the previous set but shorter than the long one; the second is longer than the previous long shot; a system of color patterns and another of movements interacts with the short-long pairs. Within such constraints chance determined which images would fill out the metrical pattern. Malcolm Brodwick designed the soundtrack on the basis of the pattern without seeing the edited film. "I consider Thom and Malcolm's film to be groundbreaking in its brilliant demon-stration of the power of a rule in constructing a film that is made of shots taken at different times and places," Fisher wrote in an 2003 statement about (). "It refuses the power of montage as that idea has been conventionally understood, only to rediscover its power in a different form, on a new plane." It exemplifies Jonas Mekas's dictum: "Chance is one of the great film editors."

Fisher's montage of nearly four hundred insert shots reveals the beauty and mystery of images otherwise veiled by the banality of commercial movie plots and trite psychology. A little more than halfway through the film, we see a hand unwinding a reel of 35mm film out of which falls packets of drugs. The dangerous secret smuggled into the ordinary paraphernalia of cinema is emblematic of the "power in a different form" Fisher has persistently sought.

The pairing of Morgan Fisher with Hollis Frampton seems ineluctable. Yet, even if Hollis Frampton hadn't screwed up his admission to Harvard by vainly bragging that he could pass the required American History exam at Phillips Academy Andover without taking the course or even opening a book – (he couldn't), and when he failed, Harvard rescinded his admission, he would not have been there when Morgan Fisher was a student. He was six years older than Fisher. Nor would he have met there the equally theory-minded, "smart-aleck" filmmaker, Tony Conrad; whose time at Harvard overlapped with Fisher's.

Fisher rarely writes or appears in public. Frampton, on the other hand, might even be a stronger writer than a filmmaker.

However, the occasion of Bruce Jenkins splendid edition of his collected writings, *On the Camera Arts and Consecutive Matters* (2015, MIT Press), provides even those quite familiar with most of Frampton's texts (I have written reviews of two of the books and tediously quoted from them for decades) to see the scope and the unity of his written work; perhaps for the first time; at least anew.

Appropriately, the book contains an implicit warning – what Maurice Blanchot called the "Noli me legere "– in the hitherto unknown, to me, interview with Adele Friedman at the Video Data Bank: "I don't want to be stuck that closely to the summary jocularities of the "Pentagram for Conjuring a Narrative" (1972; p. 187). In that article, Frampton had posited narrative as a universal aspect of film just as impishly as Fisher made the claim for synchronized sound.

What lessons can be taken from this abjuration of so crucial a theoretical text? (1) that Frampton wrote occasional essays, not a systematic theoretical discourse; (2) that they presented his thought in process rather than a range of closely reasoned conclusions; (3) that the author was an ironist whose texts were never meant to be taken literally. Yet Frampton did not emend his text when he came to reprint it in *Circles of Confusion* (1983, Visual Studies Workshop). He might even had omitted it (to our great loss). The answer seems to be that "When it comes to practically everything, we seem to be of two minds." (p. 48) He invoked the dichotomies, polarities, dualities: Left brain – right brain – of Julian Jaynes' *The Origin of Consciousness in the Breakdown of the Bicameral Mind* (1976). This seems to underpin the fundamental dichotomy of Frampton's book: *Language/ Image*.

In Frampton's critique of Abstract Expressionism and Stan Brakhage, the possibility arises of a convergence that he blesses with the rare epithet "Absolute" (recalling that he astonishingly places the conventionally Lutheran Hegel in Limbo as a "virtuous pagan" along with Aristotle, Weston and Emperor Ch'in in whose company he "should hope to spend the balance of eternity" [p. 88]); In "Impromptus on Edward Weston" he writes of "those

absolute names of things that are identical with things themselves" (p.81) We also read of the Absolute Present (p. 36) which
bifurcates into Conjecture/ Memory.

One side of his dichotomy points toward death, the other
toward birth. But to return to the opposition of Name and Thing,
it would be a tentative polarity related to Whitehead's distinction
between Eternal Object and Event (p. 80): that is a dubious, or
inventive reading of *Process and Reality* (1929) (and/or *Science and
the Modern World* [1925]) identifying language as the prime
example of an "idea" with "eternal object" and things with
"events." Weston himself appears in a Frampton text as a paragon
of contradiction: at once the splendid carnal parent, and a
crippling intellectual parent (p. 86), ultimately a "chimera" of
Venus Genetrix and Tim Finnegan, metonymies for Lucretius and
Joyce.   Frampton claimed: "The great natural poem about
anything was its *name*." *Finnegans Wake* is also a "name" for
something that *has no other name*." (p. 157). I propose "Splendid
carnal parent/ crippling intellectual parent" may be a chiastic
metalepsis for Frampton's own crippling psychotic mother and
splendid intellectual father.

Like Fisher his 'poisonous wit' abuts on 'jocular compassion.'
Science and Art are the two hopelessly ambiguous words of
"Digressions on the Photographic Agony" (p. 11) where both
sexuality and art seem to be defenses against the certainty of
death. (p. 36)

The juxtaposition of Eros and Thanatos (p. 50) ultimately
comes from Herbert Marcuse whose *Eros and Civilization* (1955)
first appeared when Frampton was 19; Norman O. Brown's *Life
against Death* (1959) came out four years later.

In a rare instance of confessional humility, he admitted, in the
text for *Hapax Legomena: (nostalgia)*, "My eye for mystery is
defective." (p. 206). In the same film he said, " I like my new
name." Regarding the identity of names and things in Weston, he
returned to the rare category of mystery: "The mysteries are
offered, but the rites of passage are withheld." (p. 81)

When he referred to his childhood inability to say "I" *in Gloria!* (1970) , his affliction was probably the echolalial pronoun reversal sometimes displayed by children with precocious linguistic ability, rather than an autistic spectrum disorder. It distantly echoes the passage in "Pentagram,": where he wrote "'I' is the English familiar name by which an unspeakably intricate network of colloidal circuits – or, as some reason, the garrulous temporary inhabitant of the nexus – addresses itself; occasionally, etiquette permitting, it even calls itself that in public.... waiting to die." (pp. 144-5) His range of references include Ray L. Birtwhistell's "The Age of a Baby" about the linguistic and perceptive effects of a schizophrenic mother (p. 47). We are also reminded of Jaynes on schizophrenia – etymologically it means "divided mind." In short, Hollis Frampton's schizophrenic mother pervades his films and his writings, despite his clever subterfuges. Too little is known of Morgan Fisher's life to encourage similar speculations.

The Puppetmaster (1993).

The Travelling Players (1975).

Hollis Frampton.

Morgan Fisher.

Peter Hutton
and
Visions in Meditation

Many of Peter Hutton's (1944-2016) films were finished before Stan Brakhage made his four *Visions in Meditation* (1989-1990). But Brakhage's innovations made Hutton's work possible from the start: *In Marin County* (1970) and *July '71 in San Francisco, Living at Beach Street, Working at Canyon Cinema, Swimming in the Valley of the Moon* (1971). Brakhage's title, *Visions in Meditation*, rephrases his elective mentor, Gertrude Stein's *Stanza in Meditation* (1932, published 1956). Hutton never refers to literature in his titles, but he did name *In Titan's Goblet* (1991) after Thomas Cole's 1833 painting of the same name.

Hutton's films celebrate places and events while Brakhage's tend to emphasize his presence in the places he films and its symbolic meaning for his life-story. This contrast is particularly true of the films Hutton made in the Hudson valley, in Iceland, China, Korea and Bangladesh in contrast to the four *Visions in Meditation*, in which Brakhage visited Eastern Canada, Maine, Mesa Verde, Carlsberg Caverns, and Taos, New Mexico.

For nearly four decades Peter Hutton has been taking the measure of the cinematic image to delimit its powers of fascination and absorption. Over those years he transformed a diaristic mode of the filmic lyric into one in which subtle fluctuations in the visible field – of light, or figures and objects in motion, or slight camera movements – configure the ecstatic concentration of the filmmaker's attention. He marshals silence and the immanent rhythms of nearly still scenes, or slow vehicular movements, to evoke the pleasures of isolation, even of loneliness. If that sounds paradoxical, it is consistent with the oxymoron or catachresis in the title he gave his third film: *Images of Asian Music (A Diary from Life 1973–74)*. Within individual shots, music or vibratory energy, becomes soundlessly pictorial: a centripetal force repeatedly concentrates the intensity of scrutiny in prolonged, suspended moments that nearly efface the subjectivity of the observer only to have it resurface in the paratactic assembly of apparently isolated shots. The persona of the filmmaker looming within Hutton's work seems to go looking for loneliness, all over the world, in fact, as if convinced that beauty reveals itself most poignantly within the modalities of alienation. This would put him at the opposite pole of Jonas Mekas, the great film diarist who can never shake off what he takes to be the painful fissions of isolation, despite the hectic whirl of social and familial life he records. In opposition to Hutton, he continually goes questing with his camera for what he has called "the ecstasy of old and new friends."

Yet, despite this difference, both Hutton and Mekas are exemplars of the Emersonian spirit of the American avant-garde cinema. Emerson's declaration in *Nature* (1836) of the simple "mechanical" means of manifesting the fundamental dualism of self and the world offers a master scenario for many of the most important films of their tradition (as I mentioned in the discussion of *Mosaik im Vertrauen*.)

> The least change in our point of view, gives the whole world a pictorial air. A man who seldom rides, needs only to get into a coach and traverse his own town, to turn the street into a puppet-show. The men, the women, – talking, running, bartering, fighting, – the earnest mechanic, the lounger, the beggar, the boys, the dogs, are unrealized at once, or, at least, wholly detached from all relation to the observer,

and seen as apparent, not substantial beings. What new thoughts are suggested by seeing a face of country quite familiar, in the rapid movement of the railroad car! Nay, the most wonted objects, (make a very slight change in the point of vision,) please us most. In a camera obscura, the butcher's cart, and the figure of one of our own family amuse us. So a portrait of a well-known face gratifies us. Turn the eyes upside down, by looking at the landscape through your legs, and how agreeable is the picture, though you have seen it any time these twenty years!

The cinematic dynamics of Marie Menken, Stan Brakhage, Ernie Gehr, and many other of Mekas's and Hutton's American peers instinctively follow the guidelines set down in this passage, as I have reiterated *ad nauseam*.

Hutton shot some films before 1971, recording in 8 mm the performances he created as a graduate student in San Francisco, and he even completed a ten-minute-long film, *In Marin County* (1970), which I have never seen. With the exclusion of these apprentice efforts, his cinematic career begins spectacularly with *July '71 in San Francisco, Living at Beach Street, Working at Canyon Cinema, Swimming in the Valley of the Moon* (1971). In fact, I can think of no school-trained avant-garde filmmaker who made so auspicious a start. (Of Hutton's significant American contemporaries, only Saul Levine, Phil Solomon, Warren Sonbert, and Leslie Thornton studied filmmaking in school, but they were slower to attract critical attention. In the generation of filmmakers before Hutton, a college degree was a rarity.)

The speed with which Hutton moved from school to prominence as a filmmaker is deceptive. He had the advantage of being a few years older than most of his fellow students in the film program at the San Francisco Art Institute (where he was awarded his MFA in 1971), but, more important, he was older because he had gone to sea first. Like *Moby-Dick's* Ishmael, who said, "A whaleship was my Yale College and my Harvard," Hutton attributes his aesthetic formation to his years in the merchant marine (intermittently between 1964 and 1974. This apprenticeship, in turn, fulfilled older fantasies, enkindled when, as a child, the future filmmaker pored over the photo album assembled by his father, himself a former sailor, from his voyages to Shanghai, Calcutta, and Angkor Wat.

July '71... spectacularly offers the gamut of vehicular motion: The first trope for the filmmaker in motion is the shadow image of his bicycle as he pedals and films at once. By the time the thirty-five-minute work ends with shots of the California hills from a flying glider, Hutton has filmed from a car and a boat as well. At one point, a man, symbolically extending the filmmaker's movements, negotiates the hills lying flat on a scooter, and in a self-portrait filmed from a static tripod, Hutton presents himself as a frizzy-haired youth, significantly doing a somersault. The mobile and inverted perspective gives the filmmaker's world Emerson's "pictorial air," as it inscribes the filmmaker's subjectivity into the traces of what he had seen. This starting point is Hutton's most social film. He made it when he lived in a commune, recording the meals, ablutions, and games of his companions.

Mekas himself and Annette Michelson were on the jury of the short-lived Yale Film Festival, which gave Hutton's film its initial accolade in 1972. The Whitney Museum of American Art programmed the film that same year, attracting the filmmaker to New York, where his older lookalike, Red Grooms, immediately hired him as the in-house filmmaker of his Ruckus studio and set him up in the basement apartment beneath it. There Hutton made his next film, *New York Near Sleep for Saskia* (1972) – Saskia is the daughter of Grooms and Mimi Gross – in which he recoiled from the visual dynamics of his earlier success in the cinematic-diary mode. Whereas *July '71...* had represented the selfhood of the artist catapulted into the world and caught up in its movements and intersubjective exchanges, *New York Near Sleep...* stilled the camera and minimized human figures to a few posed, static shots. Hutton told the journal *Satori*:

> I went from this wonderful expressive life in California to a dark,

dank, grimy, rat-infested cellar in New York. It was like solitary confinement. But in that confinement I started really focusing on much more subtle notions of what the image was or what film was... I started paying more attention to how light moves through spaces and just reducing film down to these very minimal kinds of concerns... There was also that Eastern idea that regardless of where you are, there's a world there in front of you and you have to just find it in those shadows and in that darkness.

Red Grooms, in clown regalia, initiates the film in its second shot, and Hutton himself, sitting in a chair on a raft, all but ends it. A telling allusion is made to the "Eastern idea" behind the film – a sense of "Buddhist" self-depletion – by the insertion of a few seconds from the end of Yasujiro Ozu's *Tokyo Story* (1953), filmed off a screen. The rest is cityscape and landscape, intercut with luminist interiors and objects awaiting human use: falling snow seen from a window, a steaming bathtub, a bottle of milk on a table, a breeze blowing through a volleyball net. Repeatedly the images suggest that the beauty and melancholy of isolated moments cannot be sustained. Before Hutton, Bruce Baillie had been the acknowledged master of a cinema in which objects and landscapes release their inherent energy when the static or slowly moving camera attempts to hold it. Perhaps in relocating from San Francisco, where Baillie's influence had been a dominant force, Hutton had weakened his resistance to that model. In *New York...* he seems to have absorbed the lessons of the colorist Baillie, transposing his mystical attention to objects and places into rich black-and-white tonalities.

"Near sleep" describes the film's mood, insofar as the waning of the filmmaker-subject coincides with a quasi-oneiric aura emanating from the catalogue of evanescent epiphanies in the film lyric. Here Hutton begins to isolate nearly all his shots by fading in and out, a repudiation of the impact of montage that he will pursue for most of his career. The consequent parataxis focuses the rhythmic elaboration on the movement (or stillness) within individual shots, intimating the narrative of an itinerant observer repeatedly arrested by vistas, configurations of light and shadow, things ready to hand, and actions in a discontinuous sequence.

As the filmmaker's alter ego, the clown mocks Hutton's earlier effort to assert his artistic persona, putting him in his place behind the camera, where compositional elegance and the beauty of light are to be his compensations for loneliness, in this and almost all the films to follow. *Near Sleep*'s concluding three shots eloquently chart the filmmaker's withdrawal. In the first he sits in a chair on a raft with his bare back to the camera. Then we see the empty chair. Finally, from a more distant perspective, we watch the landscape from the apparently empty raft, which slowly drifts, tethered, on the pond.

In Brakhage's films the automobile is the primary agent of vehicular movement, but for Hutton it was a boat. Before accepting the style of *New York, Near Sleep…* as his permanent mode, Hutton attempted a synthesis of it and *July '71…* In *Images of Asian Music,* he returned to the diary form and to his life at sea. Living in Bangkok in 1973 and 1974 with stints as a merchant seaman, he recorded moments of his daily life at sea and on land. The film opens on an Indonesian freighter, alternating images of the moving ship from the perspective of the solitary filmmaker with sequences of his engagement with the crew, including a cockfight they staged. At the end of a revealing interview with critic Scott MacDonald in 1995, Hutton spoke of the influence on his art of his work as a sailor:

> One of the great revelations of traveling by sea is how slow it is compared to airplane or even train travel. You can actually go backwards in time on a ship, you can sail into a storm and make no headway… One of the exhilarating and terrifying aspects of traveling by sea is the vulnerability you feel and the fact that you're not isolated from nature, but are rather in the heart of nature itself… I was up on the bow of the ship late at night, probably around three in the morning. It was completely dark: the sky was clouded up so there were no stars or moon to illuminate anything. All of a sudden I felt the temperature change… It was like going into an inkwell, and I had this revelation that there were all these declensions of darkness that I

hadn't been aware of. Pretty soon it started to rain and the seas kicked up rather dramatically and the mate on the bridge shined a light down and told me to come up. As I was turning around, a big wave dipped over the bow. It could have washed me over. I scurried up to the bridge and continued to observe the storm from up there... Being on the ship forced me to slow down and allowed me to take time to look.

Moments wrested from the press of time and images of threatening or superabundant nature occur in the film, but their integration into the evenly paced flow of sensual discoveries divests them of dramatic emphasis: Waves breaking over the bow of a ship carry no more or less weight than a coffee mug resting by the vessel's side rail on a calm day. Hutton doesn't appear in *Images of Asian Music,* but the camera indicates his presence interacting with the crew and gazing at the sea. The subjective movement culminates in a rickshaw ride through the streets of the Cambodian capital, Phnom Penh. Subsequently, the camera stills itself in rapturous contemplation of the Southeast Asian landscape of temples, rivers, and jungles, or of the light falling on the meager furnishings of his hotel room.

When he returned to America, Hutton took a series of teaching positions and fellowships that determined his creative geography for at least twenty years. While at Hampshire College, in Amherst, Massachusetts, he made *Florence* (1975), an invocation of the nearby town in which he lived when not in Manhattan, where he was completing *New York Portrait, Part I* (1976–77), the first of what he initially thought would be a ten-part series. Teaching at Harvard, he finished *Boston Fire* (1978) and *New York Portrait, Part II* (1980–81). As the guest of Hungary's Béla Balázs Studio, he translated his unique urban vision into *Budapest Portrait (Memories of a City)* (1984–86). When Hutton accepted a permanent position at Bard College, in Annandale-on-Hudson, New York, he fixed his attention on the Hudson Valley, making *Landscape (for Manon)* (1986–87), *In Titan's Goblet* (1991), and *Study of a River* (1994–96). During those years he also brought to a close his ambitious series with *New York Portrait, Part III* (1990), and, accepting another invitation to film in eastern Europe, he made *Lodz Symphony* (1991–93).

With his masterful three-part *New York Portrait*, Hutton achieved maturity as a filmmaker. In these urban meditations, he cultivates a nostalgia for loneliness and a melancholic poetry immanent, but repressed, in his earlier work. Abandoning the alternating rhythms of engagement with others and contemplative isolation that oscillate through *July '71* and *Images of Asian Music*, he gradually moves from the observation of atmospheric conditions, the flight patterns of birds, and glimpses of isolated figures in the nearly empty city of *Part I*, to snow blowing on the beach at Coney Island, sleeping tramps, flooded streets, and the slow passage of the Goodyear blimp through the skyline of *Part II*, while *Part III* abstracts and distills the imagery of the earlier sections and culminates in a sequence showing a man wounded or dead on the street.

Those shots of the man on the sidewalk, with a small crowd gathering to watch the paramedics attending to him and finally carrying him on a stretcher to an ambulance, like many in the series, were photographed from a rooftop, high above, so that the film's final image of a lone, hooded man on the edge of a roof stands in for the unseen filmmaker. Hutton's vision of New York resonates with the overwhelming melancholy evoked in the comic strip Julius Knipl, Real Estate Photographer of his friend Ben Katchor. Hutton's camera sucks in the atmosphere of a place he observes, to make palpable the lonesomeness he craves. I suspect his experience as a twin, which can deprive a child of the pleasures of isolation, may have contributed to the filmmaker's aesthetic, his persistent quest, in film after film, to transform quiet and loneliness into pictorial beauty. In his two films of Eastern European cities, *Budapest Portrait* and *Lodz Symphony*, he discovers even deeper pockets of sadness than he found in *New York*.

By the time he made the city portraits, Hutton had ceased to be a cinematic diarist, for there is very little of his daily life in his mature work. Seeing the films, one wouldn't know he was married twice and raised a daughter, although her name appears in the titular dedication of his exquisite *Landscape (for Manon),* the first of his explorations of the landscapes of the Hudson River valley that would dominate his career for two decades. The shift of subject and mood, from the lyrics of urban isolation to the ambivalent contemplation of light as it strikes the sylvan environment and the industrial development of the river, reflected his settled life as a permanent member of the Bard College faculty. He successfully transferred the wonder he had conveyed in shooting the forests and cities of Southeast Asia to the trees, bridges, factories, and cliffs of New York State while adapting the dynamics of filming at sea to the gentler rhythms of the barges and tugboats that carried him up and down the river; for he used his considerable personal charm and his experience at sea to strike up acquaintance with river pilots and bridge keepers and thereby gain extraordinary access to vantage points for filming.

With the title *In Titan's Goblet,* he pays homage to Thomas Cole, the master of the nineteenth-century Hudson River School, whose eponymous 1833 painting depicts a monumental drinking cup, so large it holds a lake with sailing vessels on it, resting on a cliff. Hutton intimates that we dwell within such a goblet, attempting to ascertain the world through smoke, mist, and clouds. He began filming it during a raging fire of automobile tires in Catskill, New York, drawing exquisite beauty from an ecological threat, as he had done in *Boston Fire.*

While rejecting the painter's mythopoeic vision, Hutton utilizes Cole's dramatic sense of scale – a recurring feature of the filmmaker's Hudson River meditations. *Landscape* opens with a shot of a train running parallel to the river, filmed from so great a distance that the train seems almost a toy. *Study of a River* continually plays with our sense of scale: Hutton films raindrops hitting a mud puddle so that they become squiggles of light in a microcosmic universe, and juxtaposes those shots with images of massive constructions filmed from a high bridge spanning the river. Even though he unconsciously repeated a startling trope from Stan Brakhage's *Creation* (1979) when he inserted an upside-down shot of ice floes, he does not invest his film with any of the mythic aura Brakhage gave his trip amid Alaskan icebergs by systematically alluding to the stages of Creation in Genesis. Instead, Hutton stresses the autonomy of each shot as a concrete locus of natural power and precarious human intervention. He is as often enthralled by the massive engineering of a ship or a bridge as he is by the energies latent in water, rock, and vegetation. The intensity of his absorption makes the individual shot a self-contained monad recalling, as critic Tom Gunning first pointed out, the initial films the Lumière brothers made at the end of the nineteenth century.

Recourse to citing films made in the first decade of cinema had been a topos of the American avant-garde cinema since Ken Jacobs initiated it with his masterpiece *Tom, Tom, the Piper's Son* (1969). Following suit, Hutton acknowledged his resignation to the history of his medium, bracketing a brief return to his rich black-and-white river imagery between the quotation of a now scratched and faded Billy Bitzer film and the lush color that will characterize his future films. The proverb from which he drew the title phrase *Time and Tide* asserts universal mortality and the inexorable demands of nature over human endeavors. Appropriately, then, it is his statement on his fate as a filmmaker. Opening with Bitzer's primitive fast-motion film of Hudson River travel from 1903, *Time and Tide* (2000-2001) marks the filmmaker's "inevitable" transition from black-and-white to color cinematography. Hutton finesses the transition spectacularly by giving us a series of images of ice-breaking from the point of view of a moving boat. Then, he follows the series by showing a seemingly vertical white expanse of the frozen river into which a rust-colored barge moves, retrospectively cueing that the ice had been filmed "in color" all along. After the barge cuts through the frozen surface and passes out of the screen, the white plane recongeals.

The next shot, of the azure and gray deck of a boat shot through a rain-spotted window, confirms that we will see the whole film in color, as it moves between Bayonne, New Jersey, and Albany, New York, from the vantage point of a tugboat. By shooting through portholes in the tug, or on overcast days when the river has a gray hue, Hutton locates zones of white, black, and gray within the colored matrix in several shots, before he fully embraces the rich hues of the riverscape and its boats.

Color plays a central role in *Two Rivers* (2001–2002), initially an installation piece combining footage shot on the Hudson and the Yangtze rivers, commissioned by Minetta Brook's Watershed Project. Hutton capitalized on a technical mistake: When he discovered that the Chinese footage he thought he had shot on black-and-white negative film stock was actually made on black-and-white reversal, he decided to go ahead and process it as negative anyway, and then had it printed on color stock, resulting in a sepia-toned print that evoked much of the traditional landscape painting on silk he had been looking at in Shanghai museums. Consequently, the saturated, predominantly blue tones of the material shot on the Hudson in the first part of the film contrast sharply with the thinner sepia of the Yangtze images, thus preserving the polarity of the initial two-screen installation.

Skagafjördur (2002–2004) and *At Sea* (2004–2007), Hutton's final works before his untimely death in 2016, bear a similar relation to *Time and Tide* that the two Eastern European city films do to the *New York Portraits*. For *Skagafjördur*, Hutton accepted an invitation from the Icelandic Film Centre (and further funding from the Whitney Museum) to film the coast of northern Iceland. In *At Sea*, he shot the construction of an immense cargo ship in Korea and the dissembling of similar vessels on the shores of Bangladesh. He composed the Icelandic film of some thirty-six static shots of sumptuous beauty, with barely a vestige of human presence. Bands of mist or clouds, and the line of the calm sea from which islands protrude like submerged cubes of rock, create strong horizontals throughout the film. The crepuscular hours of filming often push the color cinematography toward the filmmaker's earlier achievements in black and white. Still, the nuances of the observer's frame of mind so subtly rendered in many of Hutton's earlier films evade *Skagafjördur* and *Two Rivers*. In these films he has been examining how the grounding of the cinematic image in color reconditions the moods in which the landscape and its objects can be apprehended.

At Sea represents a departure from his previous work in several ways. Hutton no longer separated the shots with fades, but cut directly, as if to accentuate the awesome labors of construction and destruction depicted in the film. He even used, for the first time, the slightest zoom movements to stress the birth of the Brobdingnagian vessel or the dangerous work of its dismembering. People abound here, dwarfed by the massive construction. In the first half of the film, they are absorbed into the color-coded mechanisms of cranes and scaffolding, and at the end they appear as threatened figures, struggling with ropes, almost as scavengers, amid the peeling and rusty ruins of the sea monsters, until in the final black-and-white images they command a human scale when they peer with curiosity into the camera lens.

Hutton's oeuvre may be divided into two categories: films of places where he lived, and places he visited. Logically the films of Poland, Hungary, Iceland, China, Korea and Bandladesh would seem to be closer to *Visions in Meditation* than the San Francisco, Western Massachusetts, New York City, and Hudson Valley films, but the opposite is true. The personal dimensions that Hutton gradually weaned from his films he shot at home occupy the center of Brakhage's work wherever he films.

If ship travel was a way of life for Hutton, boats were tourist vehicles for Brakhage. He took shots of the Seine and its banks in *The Dead* (1960) and constructed the whole of *Creation* (1979) round a boat tour of Alaskan glaciers he took with his first wife, Jane. But he didn't reveal that she accompanied him until late in the film, when it came as a mild shock. The delay is perfectly logical because the filmmaker played off the narrative sequence of the opening of Genesis, showing earth and sky, land and water first, then vegetation and fauna in order. In Genesis the creation of Eve came last, an afterthought to please Adam. Thus, Brakhage held back the presence of Jane until quite late in the film. *Creation* suggests that all the elements of Genesis were always co-present but that the Biblical author, the so-called Jahwist, temporalized them for the sake of drama.

Marilyn Jull traveled with Brakhage through the making of *Visions in Meditation*, but she is not seen because of the pre-nuptial arrangement she required, Emöke Simon ends her essay on *Visions in Meditation 1*, by treating the signs of an accomplice to the making of the film:

> Brakhage's shots, the framing and montage invent a language through which [the vibratory] movement unfolds its many aspects. Movement towards the matter which releases composition of its pre-established hierarchies multiplies points of view and thus decenters the image, marks the capacity of film to transcend representation, that is to say a mediated mode of perception and to constantly re-enact the possibility of movement as an immediate mode of translating a constantly moving reality, the vibration of immediacy. The conditions seem necessary to open an "inner field," in between movement-image and time-image, in between subjectivity and objectivity, where image in meditation can take shape. The spectator is thus invited to meditate, and why not, in a playful manner, to participate in the process of actualization of the virtual narrative possibilities these images carry. One may thus take pleasure in asking, along with the principal question of "who is watching?" a series of questions that these images suggest in the context of the virtuality of fiction: "who is living in the house?" "who are the people represented in the photos?" "who is driving the car and where to?" "where are the people absent from the hotel room?" Thus framing and reframing the image in meditation would result in framing and reframing the narrative structures and may endow Brakhage's film with a condensed narrative core in quest of its own accomplishment through the spectator's playful meditative participation.

In her Deleuzian enthusiasm for the "vibratory" movements in the film, Simon neglected to mention that *Vision in Meditation 1* is the happiest of the four parts. It not only lacks the terrifying guilt of the second part, the anxious liberation of the third, or the melancholy nostalgia of the final part, but radiates a joyous mood. The answer to her last two questions would have to be Marilyn Jull Brakhage. I suspect that what she takes to be "the house" might actually be a New England or Canadian Inn where the filmmaker would have happily come upon the owner's wall of ancestral photographs.

The Last Temptation of Christ
and
Crimes and Misdemeanors

'God has just such gladness every time he sees from heaven that a sinner is praying to Him with all his heart, as a mother has when she sees the first smile on her baby's face.' That was what the woman said to me almost in those words, this deep, subtle and truly religious thought – a thought in which the essence of Christianity finds expression, that is the whole conception of God as our Father and of God's gladness in man, like a father's in his own child – the fundamental idea of Christ!...The essence of religious feeling does not come under any sort of reasoning or atheism, and has nothing to do with any crimes or misdemeanors.

Dostoevsky, *The Idiot*.

The New York Times called upon the maverick Catholic priest, Andrew Greeley, a sociologist and popular novelist, to comment upon the theological orthodoxy of Martin Scorsese's *The Last Temptation of Christ* (1988) the week of its controversial opening in 1988. Apparently pleased by this variation of film journalism, the same Sunday "Arts and Leisure" section responded a year later to the characterization of a rabbi in Woody Allen's *Crimes and Misdemeanors* (1989) with an ecumenical and interdisciplinary invitation to a rabbi (Eugene B. Borowitz), a Lutheran theologian (James Nuechterlein) and an English professor (Mary Erler) to situate the theology of the film.

It turns out that these are two unusually impressive films, among the dozen or so best commercially distributed feature films made in America in the Eighties, and certainly the only two in that select company with overt religious themes. Did the *Times* staff realize this immediately and award them the measure of "expert" scrutiny normally reserved for the Sunday book reviews? That was certainly not their deliberate strategy.

The stage was set by the fundamentalist fury over Scorsese's visualization of Kazantzakis's fantasy of a connubial episode in the life of Christ, which included Catholic television's Mother Angelica warning the faithful that they risked eternal damnation if they saw the film. Father Greeley conveniently provided a counterargument: the film's detractors are themselves heretics, he wittily demonstrated; they have fallen into Docetism, the third century error of taking Jesus as wholly divine. Then with considerable justification he faults both Kazantzakis and Scorsese for not taking the sensual Jesus seriously enough; he calls them modern Manicheans. It is a charming picture of the primitive Church gone astray inside and on the streets around New York's Ziegfield Theater's spacious cavern and enormous screen.

The success of the *Times*'s editorial ploy in this case may have inspired the weaker attempt to repeat it with the ecumenical synod over Allen's film. But none of the voices are as assured as Greeley's had been; they lack the clearly delineated controversy which had been his polemical springboard. In *Crimes and Misdemneanors* a rich Jewish ophthalmologist, Judah Rosenthal, finds a measure of peace and renewed conjugal happiness after having his troublesome mistress killed; to make matters worse there is a rabbi, as sweet as baklava, who goes blind. It has been at least thirty years since the Legion of Decency could halt the exhibition of a film in which a criminal went unpunished. So pervasive had been the terror of those moral monitors that even Hitchcock had prepared, but was not forced to include, an alternative ending to his 1958 *Vertigo* in which the protagonist hears over the radio that the man who victimized him had been arrested in Europe. Neither Nuechterlein's evocation of Hannah Arendt's recognition of the banality of evil and the modernist intellectual's unsatisfied will to believe, nor Erler's dissenting conclusion that, lacking the sublimity called for by his theme, Allen ends up suggesting, perhaps unwillingly, that love is an avoidance of ethics, quite focusses on the disturbing uniqueness of the film that elicited so unconventional a critical forum in the first place. Rabbi Borowitz suggestively aligned the film with the prophetic skepticism of Ecclesiastes, but quickly fled from his own insight into a search for signs of hope in the film.

The strength and scandal of Scorsese's film turns upon the intensity with which he focused on the theology of election, or rather how he channeled the problem of Jesus's calling from Kazantzakis' novel into a meditation on the limitations of cinematic representation. In the Gospels Jesus's election is never qualified: the Father's voice "from the heavens" confirms John's reluctant baptism – "Thou art my beloved Son; in thee I am well pleased." Mark makes this his starting point; Matthew sets it up with a genealogy linking Jesus to Adam through David, and a brief birth narrative. Luke extends and elaborates on the magical birth, and John follows Mark.

Rejecting even the studied ambiguities of the Greek novel in which a welter of miraculous effects and noises smother the words of the heavenly benediction to Jesus as well as the Baptist and his followers, Scorsese suppresses the heavenly voice utterly. Unfortunately, his remarkable gift for images, never stronger or more self-conscious than in this film, failed him in the Baptism episode. The gyrating nudes who follow the nearly psychotic Baptist – an interesting characterization by André Gregory -- look like a skinny-dipping party who found the waters chillier than they expected.

Scorsese's Jesus must lack the Father's confirmation of his ministry in order for the agony of election to play out its tensions until the final shot of the film. Therefore, there can be no

Transfiguration, the second moment of divine intervention in the synoptic Gospels. Finally, both film and novel end with the death on the cross. The resurrection, the prime event in the Gospel narratives, is foreclosed. Willem Dafoe plays a tortured Jesus whose obsessive self-doubts are relieved by equally disturbing manic moments in which he asserts his divinity. But the three Gospel guarantees of that divinity can have no place in the film. His intermittent voice-over confesses his painful uncertainty of his authority: "What if I say the wrong thing? What if I say the *right* thing?"

Yet despite the silence of the Father, miracles abound. From the very moment of its origin nearly one-hundred-and-forty years ago, the cinema has abetted pious illusionists in visualizing miracles. Georges Méliès, a prestidigitator who invented a vast imaginative tropology for the nascent cinema (to whom Scorsese devoted the film, *Hugo* [2011]), quickly discovered that by momentarily halting the recording of a shot, a prop could be added or removed from a scene to create a spectacular manifestation or disappearance. "The Temptations of Saint Anthony" was a popular film theme before the First World War.

No religious "epic" has achieved more than Scorsese with cinema's facility for staging spectacular epiphanies and transformations. His Jesus is a prolific magician, arrogantly cocksure in turning water to wine at the marriage in Cana, astonished and frightened at his raising of Lazarus, but most vividly fascinated with his mythopoeic power when, with the slightest hint from Kazantzakis, and no Gospel justification, he pulls out and offers his beating heart to his disciples.

The filmmakers lavished care on the rich visual texture of the film, in which the miracles are thoroughly integrated. Kazant-zakis' novel gave Scorsese the basis for extending the spiritual apprenticeship of Jesus through a series of encounters and visions in the desert which determine the cinematic style of the miracles and the imagery of the Passion. The stark ashen huts of a "monastery" of desert hermits foreshadows the more violent emergence of a legion of possessed paralytics from fissures in the ground; while the slow-motion struggle of their exorcistic wrestling match with Jesus, in turn, looks forward to an even slower shot of his carrying the beam of his cross amid a mocking crowd, in meticulous imitation of a painting of the same moment of the *via crucis* by Bosch. (Interestingly, it looks back as well to the slow-motion battering of Jake LaMotta in *Raging Bull.*)

At the center of the film, as its title suggests, the canonical three temptations in desert – to turn stone to bread, to throw himself from the mountain to be saved by angels, and to bow before Satan for worldly power – expand to include a fourth just before his death on the cross in which he would be rescued to deny his divinity and mission and to live out a family life. Even the three temptations in the desert have been restructured by Kazantzakis to lead into the last temptation. As Scorsese represents them, a snake with the voice of Mary Magdalene offers him love. In the temptation on the cross he will marry her and then, after her death, have children by Mary and Martha in a *ménage à trois*. A lion speaking as Judas, here a revolutionary Zealot continually exhorting Jesus to insurrection against Roman rule, appears as Jesus' heart bent on conquest. In one of the film's finest moments this encounter evokes Henri Rousseau's "Sleeping Gypsy." Finally, a talking flame, rather disappointingly resembling a gas jet, taunts him with his desire since childhood to be made God. The inventive phantasmagoria immediately recovers its strength with the sudden manifestation of a tree bearing bleeding fruit and an appearance of the Baptist to pass on his axe to Jesus. With it, he chops down the Edenic tree.

Throughout the film the exquisite imagistic invention and the well-chosen North African landscapes run counter to problems inescapably posed by the presence of familiar professional actors in the well-known roles. At one extreme, Harvey Keitel's relentlessly angry Judas and the tattooed Magdalene of Barbara Hershey are so ridiculous they call to mind the usual absurdities of Hollywood spectacles. At another, the minor roles of André

Gregory (the Baptist), David Bowie (Pilate), and Harry Dean Stanton (Paul) enhance the film with suggestions of the Dionysian in avant-garde theater, the narcissistic solipsism of musical stardom, and the borderline madness of film noir.

The very useful interview volume, *Scorsese on Scorsese* (edited by David Thompson and Ian Christie, New York: Faber and Faber, 1989) documents the pictorial and cinematic sources of the film. The remarks the director made in 1987 on his experience of religious epics are all the more revealing because they elaborate on opinions elliptically expressed by the protagonists of his first feature film, *Who's That Knocking at My Door?* (1969):

> All the religious movies I saw and loved as a kid, such as *The Robe* and *Quo Vadis?*, were more about spectacle and epic film-making than religion...[In Ray's *King of Kings*] Jeffrey Hunter was almost like a pin-up...Using a movie star for Jesus, they aren't able to deal completely with the human side...The film is full-blown Hollywood, very emphatic and vulgar...The biblical film that made the biggest impact on me, when I was at film school, was Pasolini's *The Gospel according to St. Matthew*...Up to that point, I had had an idea to do a film on Jesus, in *cinéma-vérité* style, in the Lower East Side of New York with everyone wearing suits...So I was moved and crushed at the same time by the Pasolini film because in a sense it was what I wanted to do...Just compare his Christ with Jeffrey Hunter. He doesn't act walking, he is walking; it's not self-conscious and yet it's very determined.

He adds that the music and the locations of Pasolini's film inspired him to follow his example, although he eventually found Morocco more suitable than southern Italy.

The transition from the penultimate moments on Calvary to the long fantasy of the "last temptation" corresponds to a central observation in Pasolini's most influential theoretical essay, "The Cinema of Poetry." There Pasolini cites the use of landscape in Bergman's *The Devil's Eye* (1960) example of the power of cinematic "prose:"

> "...when Don Giovanni and Pablo leave [Hell] after three hundred

years, and we see the world once again, the apparition of the world –
something so extraordinary – is presented by Bergman as a 'long
shot' of the two protagonists in a somewhat wild stretch of
springtime country landscape, one or two extremely ordinary 'closeups, and a great 'establishing shot' of a Swedish panorama of disturbing beauty in its transparent and humble insignificance. The
camera was still; it framed those images in an absolutely normal
manner. It was not felt."

Scorsese achieves a parallel effect with a long shot of a
landscape more verdant than those to which the film had
accustomed us, Jesus passes into this richer zone as soon as the
'Angel' (taken almost directly from *Il vangelo secondo Mattheo*,
instead of the beautiful, winged boy of Kazantzakis' novel)
rescues or tempts him from the Cross. Language supports and
sustains the subtle chromatic intensification as the Angel explains
that the landscape he sees is not Heaven but the earth which even
angels often envy, and that the kingdom of Heaven is actually
"harmony between the earth and the heart."

To a great extent the acting of *The Last Temptation of Christ* is
"more about spectacle and epic filmmaking" than Scorsese
acknowledges in his comparison of his film to those of the
Hollywood tradition. His Judas is a version of Nicholas Ray's
Barabbas. If Scorsese had followed Pier Paolo Pasolini's lead by
casting the film with amateurs he would have had to sacrifice
much of the histrionic and intersubjective dynamics that
contribute to the psychological portrait of Jesus. Dafoe's Jesus
begins as a neurotic loner forced into a mission in order to correct
the cruel evils he encounters. But he emerges from the desert
imbued with a rhetoric of violence, aggressively gathering a
ragtag following, disturbingly like a contemporary cult leader, for
his assault on Jerusalem where he runs amok amid the
moneychangers of the Temple and openly asserts his divinity.

Yet even during his entry into Jerusalem he lacks confidence:
"Lord, I hope this is what you want." As if to reassure him, with
miraculous prophecy, he receives stigmata, which open again in
grizzly literalization during the Words of institution. In traditional

Christian imagery stigmata are signs of the repetition of Christ's suffering, holy marks of the *imitatio Christi*. Although they are utterly out of place in a narrative of the Passion – because they undercut the dramatic moment of human suffering – the stigmata provide us with an interesting clue to the oddity of the film's genre. It is a work of cinematic hagiography closer to Dreyer's *La passion de Jeanne d'Arc*, Bresson's *Le journal d'un curé de compagne*, [*Diary of a Country Priest* (1954)] and Pasolini's *Accatone* (1968) than to Biblical epics. Like these films, *The Last Temptation of Christ* describes the inescapable confrontation with death of a figure reluctantly marked by the signs and form of the Gospels' Passion narratives. That is why Scorsese's Jesus seems so off key when he asserts his divinity.

Dreyer had entitled his last silent film *The Passion of Joan of Arc* to highlight the correspondence between the stages of her trial and immolation and the passion narratives of the New Testament. Her frightened and hesitant acceptance of her martyrdom, however, is closer to Scorsese's narrative than to the Biblical film models. Bresson's adaptation of Bernanos' novel eliminates much of the novelistic texture in which the author contrasted the naive priest, dying of stomach cancer, to the petty and sordid lives of his parishioners and fellow clergy. The film-maker's concentration brings to the fore signs of the priest's unconscious repetition of the passion, most notably when an otherwise rebellious young pupil washes his mud-splattered face as a figuration of Veronica's veil, an extra-biblical "station of the cross." *Accatone*, Pasolini's first film, mediated by an allusion to Dante's Bounconte Montefeltro (*Purgatorio V*) who was saved at the last moment of his life, charts the last days of a Roman pimp whose self-interested decisions bring him surprisingly to a state of grace.

Actually, the confusions of vocation and the surprises of fate were determinate, if occulted, themes in two of s Scorsese's strongest films, *Mean Streets* (1973) and *Raging Bull* (1980). In the former he successfully hid its Bressonian determinism in the title sequence, as if he were wary of losing both his audience and his backers by making the "religious" import of the film overt. Yet this exuberant study of fledgling gangsters begins before the titles in blackness with a spiritual challenge as Charlie's (Harvey Keitel) voiceover declares: "You don't make up for your sins in church; you do it in the streets; you do it at home. The rest is bullshit, and you know it." Or perhaps it is Scorsese's voice announcing what he reaffirmed fourteen years later, in virtually the same words, as the film's moral:

> My voice is intercut with Harvey's throughout the film, and for me that was a way to try to come to terms with myself, trying to redeem myself. It's very easy to discipline oneself to go to Mass on Sunday mornings. That's not redemption for me: it's how you live, how you deal with other people, whether it be in the streets, at home or in the office. (p. 48)

Charlie is the central figure of four friends whom the filmmaker introduced by short vignettes immediately following the titles: Tony [David Proval] runs a small nightclub; Michael [Richard Romanus] is a lone-shark and dealer in stolen goods; Johnny Boy [Robert Di Niro] exhibits his impulsive destructiveness by blowing up a mailbox; finally, Charlie is seen in church. Leaving confession, he holds his finger over a votive candle. His voiceover meditates on the "pain of Hell: The burst from a lighted match magnified a million times: Infinite. Now you don't fuck around with the infinite."

Taking his cue from Kenneth Anger's short film *Scorpio Rising* (1963), Scorsese structured a number of episodes around the quotation of a hit song on the soundtrack. The opening is particularly subtle; for the continuity of the music softens the disjunctive fusion of three temporal moments: Charlie's entry into the club; his spontaneous dancing on stage during the act of a young black stripper, Diane (Jeannie Bell); holding his finger over a match; and his later moment of fantasizing about Diane from his front-row table. The fluid transitions of separate times immediately establish the club as the habitual site of the interaction of the four friends and Charlie's iterative behavior as characteristic of his nightly routine.

At the climax of the film Charlie and his secret paramour Teresa (Amy Robinson) have to drive the obsessive debtor and welsher Johnny Boy out of New York to protect him from the revenge of Michael. As Michael and a young hitman pursue them, and eventually manage to shoot Johnny Boy, the montage reminds us that this confluence of dramatic urgencies has forced Charlie to stand up Diane on a date determined much earlier in the film. This time the well delineated characters of Amy, Tony, Michael, and above all Johnny Boy have taken us far from the opening spiritual challenge and the figuration of habitual patterns of fantasy and exhibitionism.

Even more remote are the opening titles, if they have not been entirely erased by the stylish and innovative unfolding of the crime film. Those titles had appeared over the projection of an eight-millimeter film. Of course, everyone in it was unfamiliar at the time, even those figures who would turn out to be central to the film. In it, we see Charlie shaking hands with a number of neighborhood businessmen and with a priest. The occasion, it seems, is the baptism of Christopher, his son and Teresa's. The titles then are an epilogue, smuggled into the opening of the film where they are likely to be missed. (And indeed, they were, if my reading of the critical literature on the film is not remiss.) Yet they make all the difference to its religious motif. Charlie's redemption was out of his hands. The pressures of a sudden and violent situation spoiled his long-fantasized date and threw him together with Amy in a chase that would eventuate in a crash and a shooting (whether or not Johnny Boy survived is undetermined). Furthermore, it had to terminate the secrecy of their relationship, which Charlie had stressed to avoid the disapproval of the Mafioso uncle for whom he collected money. The home movie elliptically attests to their marriage, parenthood, and Charlie's integration into the community.

While encouraging viewers to see *Mean Streets* as a traditional crime film, enlivened by a very energetic moving camera and method acting, the initially indecipherable fusion of prologue and epilogue allows a very different narrative to coexist with it. In this second narrative Bresson provided the models with his *Un condamné a mort s'est echappé* [*A Man Escaped*] (1957) (where the title gives away the conclusion) and his *Pickpocket* (1957) (a version of Dostoyevsky's *Crime and Punishment* in which the failure of his criminal aspirations opens a blocked man to love).

The filmic signs that permit *Mean Streets* to be viewed as either a spiritual biography or a crime film, similarly cast *Raging Bull* in alternate genres: although it is obviously akin to many boxing films, it is also a drama of redemption through pain and degradation. In this case the final title underlines the Christological analogy. Line by line, the words of John's Gospel, chapter nine, lines 24 and 25, appear on the screen, followed by a dedication of the film in memory of Haig Manoogian, the head of NYU's Institute of Film and Television who had gone to extraordinary lengths to help Scorsese after he graduated. We may take the Biblical citation as a reference to the dedication, where it is indeed appropriate; for John narrates the hostile interrogation by Pharisees of a man cured of blindness. It ends: "All I know is this: Once I was blind and now I can see." Manoogian died just before the film was finished. Therefore, there are good reasons to separate the content of the film from the dedication. But I cannot disassociate the quoted passage from its context, particularly the Pharisees spurning of the witness: "'Thou wast altogether born in sins, and dost thou teach us?' And they turned him out."

The citation that ambiguously bridges the film's narrative to its dedication is not the only indication of an exemplary parable inscribed in his biography of Jake La Motta [played by Robert Di Niro]. The film's music, from the Intermezzo of Mascagni's *Cavalleria Rusticana* hints that La Motta's story of family violence and excesses of professional sadism and masochism is not only operatic, but even a version of the melodrama of betrayal, jealousy, and pointless violence which culminates in Turridu's fatal knife fight with Alfio. There is a difference: LaMotta does not die in the ring. After letting Sugar Ray Robinson maul him – the film-maker dwells on slow-motion shots of blood spouting from his eyes and face and ends the scene with an unforgettable image of blood dripping from the ropes of the ring – La Motta descends from owning a nightclub, to prison (for serving minors) and the loss of his family; a pathetic attempt at being a comedian precedes a more successful act reciting bits of Shakespeare, *On the Waterfront*, and his own autobiographical jingles.

According to Scorsese, he came to make the film only "after having gone through a similar experience" (pp. 76-77), following the financial failure of his *New York, New York* (1977). The final phrase of La Motta's rhyme – "That's entertainment!" – points both to the grim commonality of prize fighting and nightclub acts and to the contradiction at the heart of Scorsese's artistic enterprise: the sort of economic success that allows a filmmaker to keep on making feature films with some degree of independence comes from genre formulas – the crime film, the boxing story – not religious parables.

As in the opening titles of *Mean Streets* "amateur" filmmaking plays a role in *Raging Bull*. To synopsize La Matta's career from the earliest flashback of 1941 to 1947 (the year he was suspended for throwing a fight) the film-maker cuts between still images of the bouts and the only images in color in the whole film, 16mm "home movie" reconstruction of La Motta's second marriage, his brother's first, his new home, and his children and his brother's playing together. Such silent, celebratory cinema promotes "documentary" illusions of the happy life for which the long "fictional" film in which they are embedded constitutes the dark truth.

In the "home movies" unedited flashes of pure color indicate their raw, or amateur, nature. Yet at the very end of *The Last Temptation of Christ* Scorsese cuts from the Cross on which Jesus cries "It is fulfilled," to color flashes from the end of camera reels.

Thus, taking over a trope from the avant-garde filmmaker Stan Brakhage, who uses it repeatedly and ended his epic *Dog Star Man* (1961-65) this way, Scorsese collapses the sacred moment with a declaration of the ephemerality of the chemistry of color film. In the film where we would least expect it, a declaration of cinematic specificity marks the end.

These three films share both a theme and a pattern. Their protagonists are all in the powerful grip of a vocation, which variously brings them to a fate they have resisted or avoided. As such they are allegories for the film-maker's obsession with his art and the unforeseen and often agonizing illuminations it has brought him.

Woody Allen is much more explicit than Scorsese in locating the persona of the filmmaker in his work. The end of *Crimes and Misdemeanors* could pass for a summary statement. As the disillusioned filmmaker, Clifford Stern (played by Allen himself) drinks alone in a reception room, the saccharine Rabbi, Ben, still upbeat despite his misfortune, dances with his daughter at her wedding. The voiceover of the philosopher Louis Levy, the subject of one of Stern's failed documentaries who may be modeled on Primo Levi, speaks the film's coda:

> We are all faced throughout our lives with agonizing decisions, moral choices. Some are on a grand scale; most of these choices are on lesser points. But we define ourselves by the choices we have made. We are, in fact, the sum total of our choices. Events unfold so unpredictably, so unfairly, human happiness doesn't seem to have been included in the design of creation. It is only we with our capacity to love that give meaning to the indifferent universe. And yet, most human beings seem to have the ability to keep trying and even to find joy in simple things, like their family, their work, and from that hope that future generations might understand more.

Corresponding to every phrase of Levy's declaration, part of a shot from the feature film we have just seen reappears. Judah Rosenthal's fatal affair with the stewardess Dolores Paley [Angelica Huston] – whom he has had murdered – represents the "grand scale;" while the engagement of the vulgar television sitcom producer, Lester [Alan Alda] to the public television employee Halley Reed [Mia Farrow] – whom Stern wanted to marry – and the memories of the moral precepts of the religious Sol Rosenthal which briefly obsess his guilty son, Judah, are the "unpredictable" and "unfair" events that puzzle the place of happiness "in the design of creation." The marriage of Ben's daughter and Stern's afternoon movie-going with his teenage niece represent the human capacity for finding "joy from simple things." Even a shot of Mussolini addressing a crowd in the Piazza Venezia, an image from Stern's subversive portrait Lester, finds its way into this finale, to emphasize that "we are... the sum total of our choices."

The clip of Mussolini, in fact, strengthens the identification of the coda with the filmic style of Stern who deflates his successful brother-in-law through montage, comparing him to the Italian dictator as well as through both dubbing – he puts his oft-repeated definition of comedy ("If it bends it's funny; if it breaks it's not") in the mouth of Francis, the Talking Mule from television – and through candid photography – he records him sexually harassing an actress.

Levy's agnostic wisdom and the authority of this terminal montage almost makes us forget the contradictions they imply. The first is obvious and surely part of Allen's strategy: Levy himself is a suicide. His note – "I've gone out the window" – brings the bitterest laugh in the film. The act itself squelches any chance Stern might have had, with Reed's help, of getting a public television airing of the film. In her words, "They love a positive subject."

Thus, the fictional Levy fails to fulfill his own valorization of human effort and modest fulfillment in the face of "the indifferent universe." But it is more interesting that Stern, with whom we necessarily identify Allen the filmmaker, if only because he plays the role in the sad-sack style of his movie persona, is a very different kind of filmmaker. As if to prove this, *Crimes and*

Misdemeanors makes more elaborate use of the long take and sequence shots than any previous Allen film. The power of montage is generally reserved for the often-remarkable shifts from Judah Rosenthal's life to Stern's. Ironically, if anyone in the film represents Woody Allen's actual position in the world, it is the unbearably smug Lester. He is rich; universities offer him honorary degrees; there are courses taught about "existential motifs in [his] situation comedies"; and, after affairs with glamorous women, he ends up with the heroine played by Mia Farrow. Like Allen, he has an obsession with the categories of comedy and tragedy. He even pontificates about the humor of Oedipus's situation, just before Allen himself began filming his comic episode *Oedipus Wrecks* for the compilation film, *New York Stories* (1989).

Actually *New York Stories* demonstrates the difference between the "religious" dimensions of Scorsese's and Allen's cinema quite clearly; they both contributed episodes. Allen's fantasy of a middle-aged lawyer (played by himself) whose mother disappears in a magic act and miraculously reappears in the skies over New York, revealing his intimate secrets until he finds and marries a "nice Jewish girl," is a sendup of Mariolatry, and as such part of his ongoing fascination with the oddities of Catholicism. As the title indicates, the film relies on psychoanalytical rather than religious principles. On the other hand, Scorsese's contribution to the same compilation film, *Life Lessons*, has no overtly religious themes or allusions; it is an episode in the career of a successful abstract painter, who uses the anxiety and pain the infidelities and disaffection of his young girlfriend, herself a fledgling painter, cause him to complete the work for a new show. Like every attempt in the commercial cinema to portray a serious painter, *Life Lessons* fails, even if heroically: the gap between the nuances of painterly discourse and the acting styles of Nick Nolte and Rosanne Arquette is as great as that between Willem Dafoe and Jesus without the mediation of a tradition of Hollywood Biblical epics; the expressionistic camera gestures of Nestor Almendros look particularly vapid in mimesis of a painter's strokes. Nevertheless, the film reasserts Scorsese's central preoccupation, the religious nature of artistic vocation. In his protagonist's words: "Your work is sacred."

Scorsese's strongest works are fictions of formation, in which a religious conviction comes with or in spite of a vocation. But Woody Allen's best films are Menippean satires, mazes in which aspirations toward tragedy and religious revelation are systematically frustrated by the self-conscious conventions of American movies. Near the end of *Crimes and Misdemeanors*, Judah Rosenthal tells Stern of his crime under the guise of describing a good plot for a murder film, in which we learn that he gradually felt relief from his guilt and obsession with "the eyes of God."

> Stern: So then his worst beliefs are realized... I would have him turn himself in, 'cause, you see, then your story assumes tragic proportions because, in the absence of a God or something, he is forced to assume responsibility himself. Then you have tragedy.
>   Rosenthal: But that's fiction; that's movies. You see too many movies. I'm talking about reality. I mean if you want a happy ending, you should go see a Hollywood movie.

The viewers are already acquainted with Stern's passion for Hollywood movies. We see him for the first time in the film watching Hitchcock's *Mr. and Mrs. Smith* (1941) with his teenage niece. The film clip that surprisingly joins the story of Stern to the initial exposition of the drama between Rosenthal and Dolores Paley seemed initially a collage analogy in a comic register to the tense scene between that couple, until a countershot of Stern in the audience retrospectively revealed that the framework had shifted. And then, for a moment, the memory of Allen's earlier *Manhattan* (1979) might encourage the suspicion that the very young companion could be his lover, grotesquely even younger than Tracy [Mariel Hemingway], the high school girl of the earlier film. Later, a similar transition is marked by a clip from *This Gun*

For Hire (1942) signaling Judah's consideration of having Dolores killed, and later still, the even greater catachresis of pivoting between the two plots with the song, "Murder, He Said" from *Happy Go Lucky* (1946), Stern's failed attempts to seduce Reed involve taking her to afternoon films, or even showing her a print of *Singin' in the Rain* (1952) on his flatbed editing machine. Finally, a viewing of a montage of "time passing" as Edward G. Robinson works in the laundry at Alcatraz in *The Last Gangster* (1937) – again seen with the niece – elliptically represents Reed's four-month absence in England (where Lester wins her).

Each quotation of a Hollywood film – nothing from *Singin' in the Rain* is seen – announces a turn from the melodrama of Dr. Rosenthal to the comedic frustrations of film-maker Stern, even though there is always a direct linkage between the themes of the popular films and Rosenthal's crime. Rosenthal intuits more than he could know of Stern's constricted sense of justice; for the filmmaker cannot escape the formulaic morality of the Hollywood "happy ending." His fascination with the "wisdom" of Levy reflects his defensive, and ultimately rancorous, critique of religion. He shows Reed a talking head of Levy who sagely observes: "In spite of millennia of efforts, we have not succeeded to create a really and entirely loving image of God." Levy's Divinity is a psychoanalytical construct.

Peter Hutton.

Visions In Meditation (1989-1990).

Crimes and Misdemeanours (1989)

The Last Temptation of Christ (1988).

Marjorie Keller
and
Birth of a Nation (by Jonas Mekas)

A somewhat more incongruous pair of filmmakers than Fisher and Frampton would be Marjorie Keller and Jonas Meklas. As I write these quasi-obituaries, of my 'best friend' and my late wife, I am well aware that between the time of writing and publication there may be several other deaths of those mentioned in this book, perhaps even of its author.

Jonas Mekas lived a long time: he died a month after his ninety-seventh birthday, on January 23, 2019. Marjorie Keller died at 43, on February 17, 1994. The vulgar American expression 'dropped dead' would be appropriate in her case. Her elderly mother discovered her body of the floor of the bathroom in her house in central Florida where she had gone for a short visit with our three-year-old twins, Miranda and Augusta Sitney, at the start of her very first academic sabbatical semester.

The local coroner could not find a cause for her death. He ruled out foul-play and suicide; and found no trace of disease. Eventually, he signed her death certificate as 'sudden coronary arrest," a meaningless periphrasis for 'her heart stopped.' My personal physician, the great diagnostician John Seed, asked if she might have had access to grapefruit juice. I told him that her parents grew grapefruit and oranges on their Florida property where she died. He speculated that taking an antihistamine pill (she had a serious cold then) with grapefruit juice might have killed her. A decade later, his theory became commonplace. Warnings against taking such pills with grapefruit juice became familiar.

At the time of her death, she was working on numerous projects. She planned to make a film about teaching our three-year-old twins how to read. She had filmed the process of making light fixtures at the Holophane Corporation – once headed by her father, Clarence Keller, then refinanced and purchased from the Johns Manville Corporation by her brother, Lee Keller; and she had begun to shoot a portrait of her friend, the painter Richard Fraenkel. It was to be her first sabbatical semester from teaching at the University of Rhode Island. She hoped to finish some of those films and make considerable progress on editing the others. At the same time, she expected to begin writing a book on a few "neglected" women avant-garde filmmakers who, like her, were of the third generation of American avant-garde filmmakers who benefitted from having some of the first and second generation as their college teachers. I recall only Abigail Child, Mary Filippo, Anne Robertson and Suki Wagner among her subjects, but she had in mind to discuss several others.

She had recently written, designed, and assembled a pop-up picture book, *The Moon on the Porch*, which she conceived the summer we rented Robert Breer's house on Block Island, just after she finished writing her dissertation, while waiting to defend it for her Ph.D. That dissertation became the basis for *The Untutored Eye*: *Childhood in the Films of Cocteau, Cornell and Brakhage* (Rutherford [N.J.]: Fairleigh Dickinson University Press/ Associated University Presses, 1986). *The Moon on the Porch* was not the only product of our annual summer rental houses (before we built our own house in Rhode Island in 1987). Her films, *Six Windows* (1976), *Green Hill* (1984), and *Private Parts* (1988) were shot at different rentals in Rhode Island.

Similarly, she shot *Daughters of Chaos* (1980) at her parents' house in Yorktown heights, N.Y. and at the wedding of a niece; *The Fallen World* (1983) on a trip we took to Rome and at her eldest sister's lake-house in Massachusetts; and *The Answering Furrow* (1985) in Mantua, Italy, the Greek island of Kea, and at her father's garden in Yorktown Heights. (Whereas Mekas never shed his childhood identity as a farmer, Keller was a gardener.) *Daughters of Chaos* took its title from John Cowper Powys' novel, *Weymouth Sands,* while Virgil's *Georgics* gave the structure as well as the title to *The Answering Furrow.*

It might seem grossly overambitious to expect to engage so many projects at once, but Marjorie Keller was extraordinarily energetic and expert at timing her tasks. She was a fulltime professor of filmmaking, film history, and photography at the University of Rhode Island while serving as the chairperson of the Board of Directors of the Filmmakers Cooperative of New York at a time when it required elaborate financial and managerial overhauling, and the founding editor of the journal *Motion Picture.* While doing all that she had succeeded in finishing *Herein* (1991), a complex 35-minute-long film about her political past and the apartment house in what was then a lower Manhattan slum where she, and filmmakers Su Friedrich, Mary Filippo, and David Geary, lived alongside Chinese, Hassidic, and alcoholic tenants. "Herein" was the opening word for the FBI files on potentially 'subversive' citizens then recently made available to the people surveilled. Hers was dozens of pages long with almost all the entries blacked out, presumably to protect the secret infiltrating agents who reported them. She had been an active organizer for the Students for a Democratic Society during the Vietnam War and had led rent strikes for oppressed tenants in Chicago, where she and her then boyfriend, the filmmaker Saul Levine, had gone to the School of the Art Institute of Chicago when they were kicked out of Tufts University for too vigorously protesting the unjust firing of an African-American secretary.

Practical politics – she had no patience for academic Marxists who preferred theory to working with the poor or oppressed.

Gardens, and above all, family, were the center of her work. She was the youngest of seven children, a beloved aunt to nearly twenty nephews and nieces. I recalled her hand-making a "cabbage patch doll" when one of her young nieces despaired because the commercial versions were sold out in a pre-Christmas frenzy, and sewing a formal tailcoat for a nephew to wear when he staged his magic tricks. The imagination and passions of children fascinated her. Thus, the cinema of childhood in the history of the avant-garde film was the natural subject for her dissertation and first book. At the time she was writing it, she was in psychoanalysis four days a week. The insights of that analysis found their way into *The Untutored Eye*. Its title comes from Stan Brakhage's *Metaphors on Vision*. At that time Brakhage's writings and films were anathema to the feminist supporters of *her* films, but she publicly and adamantly acknowledged her debts to Brakhage and her admiration of his films, if not of his patriarchal behavior and remarks.

Brakhage insisted upon certain biological and psychological differences between men and women; he even cited an obscure study by Ray L. Birdwhistell that mothers unconsciously train their infant sons to employ different eye movements and scansions than their daughters. (I have never found that article.) Nevertheless, Brakhage supported several women filmmakers and acknowledged Marie Menken as the greatest influence on his style. Keller willingly accepted the idea of gender differences but she vehemently rejected notions of female inferiority in making or appreciating art. She admired Mekas's films and wrote on an essay on his relation to his mother for David James's *To Free the Cinema: Jonas Mekas and the New York Underground* (New York: Oxford University Press, 2020).

When I saw Mekas's *Birth of a Nation* (1997) for the first time. I disliked the title. I was too much of a Latinist to think of the community of international filmmakers as a *nation*. A nation is made up of people born [*natus*] the same place, often speaking a language unique to that place. I believed Mekas's nation always was Lithuania even though he lived most of his very long life in the United States. Now I realize that its title responds to the films of its time that speculated on national identity and history: *O Thiassos*, *The Puppetmaster*, et alia, as I discussed in a previous chapter of this book. Mekas firmly believed that filmmakers transcended nationalism.

Upon re-seeing the film after Mekas's death, I am struck first of all by how young we all were when he made it, and by how many of the characters in its immense cast are now dead. At first, I saw it as a catalogue of filmmakers and people associated with them. I thought it was merely another effort by Mekas to use up the immense storehouse of footage he had accumulated. I hadn't been deeply moved by any of the films he had made in the previous two decades, and I awaited something like his late masterpiece, *As I Was Moving Ahead Occasionally, I Saw Brief Glimpse of Beauty* (2000). (Yet I was unprepared for its towering greatness when he first showed it to me.) Today, *Birth of a Nation* seems very different, and I can even accept the title, as an acknowledgement that the avant garde film community were born native to their fates.

The first time, I was so eager to identify everyone that I missed the structure of the film. For the most part, it records, out of chronological order, the meetings of filmmakers from the perspective of a naïve Parzifal figure, as if they possessed the Holy Grail. I am in it frequently, but merely by accident, since Jonas and I lived in the same city during the thirty years it was filmed, and we shared many friends. We were usually together when he was in New York. But Hollis Melton, his wife, and their children, Oona (and later, Sebastian), were with him more often and consequently they are in the film more than I am. The genuinely important figures are the ones who are the subjects of its editing. I would call them "motives for montage." The filmmaker combines several shots of them in a sequence to create portraits. Sometimes he even disperses the portraits at different times in the film. We see Kubelka, Harry Smith, Ken Jacobs and his family, Brakhage, Barbara Rubin, Broughton, McBride, Hanoun, Anger, and Langlois as "motives for montage." Only once does he cut from Oona – to another shot of her violin practice with her mother.

As for the title, Mekas had tremendous enthusiasm for Griffith's film. He gave Seymour Stern an entire issue of *Film Culture* to write about it and document it. Its perversion of American history and sentimentality, which disgusted me, did not have the same effect on him; he was thrilled by Griffith's formal achievements and the scope of his film. The heritage of slavery was not part of his history. He did not understand American racism.

In the literal sense, his one nation was Lithuania. But it was scattered, in exile in the New World, with a strong base in Soviet captivity. Likewise, the avant-garde filmmaking community had accepted (even adored) him in ways that the United States didn't until the 21st Century. It too was internationally dispersed, with a strong base in New York.

I was incapable of identifying with my image in the film because of its lack of relevant contextual events. *Walden* and *As I Was Moving Ahead...* are filled with events I recall because I participated in some of them. I do not recall most of the times I appear in *Birth of a Nation*, despite several viewings.

Frequently, I was a guest at the Mekas dinner table when filmmaker-friends visited, and I appear when the Selection Committee of Anthology Film Archives met to choose films for the Essential Cinema collection in 1969 and 1970. I cannot remember why I was dancing, solo, in the street, later in the film. Mekas carried his camera with him at all times. But he did not bring lights. So, many of the indoor scenes are so dark it is hard to see the people or to identify the places they are in. Thus, I may be in the film more than I know.

If the Sixties was the greatest period of creative invention in the American avant-garde cinema, the Seventies was the time of its institutionalization. During that decade, Mekas had to appear at many of the conferences in the United States and in Europe that I shunned. The advantage he found was that filmmakers from all over gather at them. Thus, he went to Hamburg for them (where he films his German TV producer, Hans Brecht, and several filmmakers), and Toulouse (in 1974), London, Toulon and Paris (in 1977 for the opening of "Une histoire du cinéma" at Musée Pompidou and other unspecified times). In the US, besides New York City, he filmed several times in both Binghamton and Buffalo (where Gerald O'Grady directed the Media Center of the University that sponsored several conferences in the Seventies, including one on Autobiography (1973), in New York, Pittsburgh (where Robert Haller and Sally Dixon ran avant-garde film showcases), and Boston, Massachusetts (for the Documentary Film Conference, 1974 at M.I.T.)

If there is an action that dominates *Birth of a Nation*, it is eating. Both in homes and at conferences people ate together. There is even a scene in New York's Puglia Restaurant, but it is too dark to be sure who was there. Mekas would film at all those dinners; and he recorded the encounters, when he met friends or filmmakers on the street, either in New York or abroad. He liked to fall behind, or run in front of, his friends to film a group heading to a restaurant or a screening. In rapid succession he offered outdoor portraits of Richter, Rossellini, Clarke, Rogosin, Baillie and Rubin before returning to Kubelka – his favorite subject in *Birth of a Nation*.

Mekas played a boyan in his room at the Chelsea Hotel and filmed George Maciunas on a rooftop. He also liked to film others shooting films, making music of even taking still photographs: e.g. Heliczer with a guitar, Kubelka with a recorder, Chikiris, Hanoun and Leacock snapping photos, Shirley Clark filming Andy Warhol and Michel Auder, and Barbara Rubin filming Ronna Page; there is even of slow pan from a Bolex camera up to Jud Yalkut holding it.

But wherever Mekas filmed one of his friends or associates, he turned from his human subject to record what attracted his attention nearby: such as, fruit, potted plants, leaves, traffic, a donkey (at Nitsch's castle in Prinzendorf, Austria), or New York as seen from high office windows. In essence, my appearances in the film are metonymic as well, insofar as I just happened to be at dinner with Broughton, Peterson, Singer and Kelman, or walked along side of Langlois, Kubelka, or Foreman, greeted Ledoux, or as a member of the Anthology Film Archives Selection Committee, talked with Michelson and Wibom, et alia.

I wish I had asked the filmmaker why he incorporated the lecture on the figure of the Fool in *Parzifal* and, erroneously, an ignorant guide claiming Christ meant "fool" [*Christos* (1 Peter 2:3) means "kind, good" not "fool" in NT Greek] in apocryphal Christian history. F.U. Ragazzi informed me that the speaker is Jean Houston. Hers is the only spoken passage in the whole film. Mekas was particularly susceptible to such pseudo-scholarly mystics and popularizers: yet her commentary during that one extended speech is as crucial to an understanding of his self-image in *Birth of a Nation* as is the penultimate sequence in which he shows himself appropriately as his own "motive for montage".

He also put the title card "Autobiography" into the montage in which he, on all fours, imitates a dog. In this film, as often elsewhere he enacts the Fool. As early as July 1963 Brakhage had scolded him for calling the Filmmakers' Cooperative "a monastery of fools." In fact, Parzifal recurs throughout the film. Ragazzi thinks that the musical score seen briefly is from Wagner's opera which Mekas excerpted on the soundtrack. He also points to the page from Wolfram von Eschenbach's medieval poem that appears several times. The film terminates with the architect, Raimund Abraham, cooking a meal "for Parzifal." Are they eating before going to Wagner's opera? I doubt it. It is more likely that Jonas thinks of himself as the Parzifal for whom Abraham prepares a roast.

All through *Birth of a Nation*, characters play and clown: Harry Smith makes a comic gesture as he gets into a cab, Taylor Mead acts scary for the Mekas children, Ken Jacobs plays with an empty frame, Jerome Hill claws the air in front of the filmmaker. The gaze of a camera itself encourages foolish play as a defense against the self-consciousness of being filmed. That may even be why I am dancing alone. Subjected to Mekas's camera-gaze the avant-garde filmmaking community may be seen as a nation of inspired fools. In this film the archetype of The Fool possesses us.

George Landow
and
Saul Levine

A somewhat less incongruous pair would be the filmmakers I am combining here, by putting together two Jewish avant-garde filmmakers from Hamden, Connecticut, George Landow and Saul Levine. The former flirted with Christian fundamentalism, while the latter, an atheist, exemplifies the pattern of a secular Leftist. Both were friends of mine for more than sixty years. George Landow was found dead in his Los Angeles apartment on June 8, 2011, at the age of sixty-six. (Levine is now in his eighties, was living in the suburbs of Boston, when I wrote this chapter.) Landow was an exceptionally private, even mysterious man, and though he was a luminary of the American avant-garde cinema, little is known of his personal life or the circumstances of his death. Shortly after hearing of his demise, I happened upon an undated letter he had sent to Stan Brakhage (presumably in the early 1970s). It appears to be a response to a request from Brakhage for a summary of his formation as an artist. He wrote:

> The biographical data which seems significant to me concerns my
> continuing attempts to satisfy my curiosity about the apparent
> absurdities of the world. Perhaps this curiosity caused me to begin to
> make art – initially taking the form of deliberately absurd responses
> to situations in which one was expected to respond in a conventional

way (though I still like the technique, the element of pride in it makes me usually refrain from using it)… Inspired by such writers as Joyce and Beckett, I thought that what I really wanted to do was write theater of the absurd type plays. Then I found myself in art school, on the road to becoming a painter – so as to be able to deal with existential material in a more concrete way – to make it visible… If this were a traditional "testimony" and a not a biographical note, I would write about how I was actually transformed through a spiritual encounter with the Messiah. I will only say that I began to understand human history in the light of the truths revealed in the scriptures and saw the resurrection as the event around which all others revolve. Making films is important to me, but I can only do it for at most about fifty more years. What is fifty years compared with all time (or no time)? If art is made in heaven (the bible tends to indicate that it is), I would like to make music for the glory of God.

The note makes no mention of the remarkable trajectory of Landow's career. He made his first films in 16mm in 1961, when he was sixteen. By the time he was twenty, he had been recognized by Jonas Mekas, in the *Village Voice*, as an original genius, and today there are some thirty works in his filmography, six in 8mm and the last four, made between 1984 and 2009, in video. Perhaps his fear of the sin of pride prevented him from bragging of his precocity and of the range of his early work. At the time he began making films, he also experimented with distorting the images he found on television (somewhat along the lines that Nam June Paik was simultaneously exploring but would not exhibit until 1963), and he performed a self-destroying film, or "concerto for projector," at Southern Connecticut State College in New Haven in 1961.

He conceived of the structural film for which he is probably best known, *Film in Which There Appear Edge Lettering, Sprocket Holes, Dirt Particles, Etc.* (1965–66), first as a found-footage loop that the projectionist would interrupt after eleven minutes with an advertisement – specifically, a shot of Rembrandt's *Syndics* as it appears inside Dutch Masters cigar boxes; later he would reconfigure the work as a two-screen piece with the image on the left flipped so that the half face at the frame edge became a third figure when the two projections overlapped. Landow's pioneering performance art was stymied in 1965 when a street action he staged at Brooklyn's Pratt Institute nearly got him expelled. Pratt was, in fact, his second college. He had started at New York University as a Classicist but left after a year. In 1993, on the threshold of middle age, he took an MFA in painting from the New York Academy of Art, where he had hoped to learn to "paint like Caravaggio." He also studied acting, guitar, and Indian classical music. None of these endeavors met with any of the success of his films, although he did manage to stage several of his plays, including "Mechanical Sensuality" (1977) and "Schwimmen mit Wimmen" (1982) at the School of the Art Institute of Chicago and elsewhere.

Recurring medical problems played a large role as shifting foci of interest in Landow's fragmented institutional life. He nearly died of colitis at sixteen (the first of many serious afflictions from what was probably as-yet-undiagnosed Crohn's disease). After months in Yale–New Haven Hospital, he had a colostomy. His several attempts to live in New York, making films and studying painting (he tried the Art Students League as well), were frustrated when ill health forced him to return repeatedly to his parents' home in Hamden, Connecticut. His desire to keep his medical problems private reinforced his constitutional secrecy; he would disappear for long periods at a time without informing anyone of his whereabouts.

We had been born in the same apartment building in New Haven, just thirty-two days apart, both the only children of parents in their late thirties. Together as teenagers we had pored over the films of Brakhage, Maya Deren, and Gregory Markopoulos; and read Joyce, Beckett, and Ionesco aloud to each other. But there were many times when he retreated into his illness and refused to see me or any of his friends. After a convalescence, he would often move to a new location, find a new – often minimal – means of making a living, sometimes change his art medium and once, his name. Later in life, complications of his digestive system forced him to retire early from his tenured position in the film department of the School of the Art Institute of Chicago.

He was even widely believed to have died shortly before his suspended work in progress *Undesirables (Condensed Version)* (1999), a satire on the pretensions of avant-garde filmmakers, screened in the 2002 New York Film Festival's Views from the Avant-Garde program. But the British curator Mark Webber would soon track him down in Deerfield Beach, Florida, where he was living with his aged mother. In 2001, he had had a stroke that disabled half his body. Although Landow was unable to attend the touring retrospective of his films that Webber organized for New York's Whitney Museum of American Art and Tate Modern, London, in 2005, Webber's efforts – which also included editing the book *Two Films by Owen Land* (Lux, 2005) – revitalized the filmmaker's enthusiasm for cinema. He managed to move to Los Angeles, where he shot and edited what would be his final work, the two-hour digital film *Dialogues, or A Waist Is a Terrible Thing to Mind* (2009), exhausting his fiscal resources. He died destitute. Barely three months before his own demise, his mother passed away just shy of her 102nd birthday, but he couldn't afford to attend her funeral.

His earliest films – *Faulty Pronoun Reference, Comparison and Punctuation of the Restrictive or Non-Restrictive Element* (1961), *Are Era* (1962), *Richard Kraft at the Playboy Club* (1963), and *Fleming Faloon* (1963–64), for instance – hold up remarkably; indeed, they look even more extraordinary after sixty years, Landow was unique in his subjects and in his relationship to the processes of filmmaking. Television, advertisements, linguistic confusions were the materials of his first films, and they remained his favorite subjects. Above all, he used cinema as a means to explore the illusory nature of images. The betrayal of his body taught him to distrust the physical world: three-dimensional space and sequential time were mere illusions to him; he saw material phenomena as muddled signs of a transcendental order. The phrase "Oh, it was a dream!" which ends *Wide Angle Saxon* (1975), bespeaks the filmmaker's sense of cinema as a tool for revealing the illusionary modality of experience. He once told me he planned a series of films to end with that expression. However, we do not hear it at the end of his next work, *On the Marriage Broker Joke as Cited by Sigmund Freud in Wit and Its Relation to the Unconscious or Can the Avant-Garde Artist Be Wholed?* (1977–79), in which a woman awakens to recite an orgasmic account of a visionary experience Mrs. Jonathan Edwards wrote up in the eighteenth century and Landow found in William James's *The Varieties of Religious Experience* (1902). He wasn't the first avant-garde filmmaker to explore the veil of illusion: Jordan Belson and Harry Smith, preceded him in that. Landow's unique contribution was to focus on the detritus of television and advertisement as the *signatura rerum* – the more banal, the more spiritually immanent, he implied.

His sense of humor was at odds with his metaphysical beliefs, as mischievously demonstrated in films such as *Thank You Jesus for the Eternal Present* (1973) and *Wide Angle Saxon*. In that autobiographical account to Brakhage, he confessed:

> I… developed the technique of fabricating fantastic stories about myself and relating them in a perfectly deadpan manner so as to convince my hearers of their authenticity. This was not done maliciously, but out of a sense of the absurdity of all phenomena and the arbitrariness of all information. This may be a form of poetry, which in Greek means making – as in "making it up." Usually it is called "lying."

This confession casts doubts on how seriously one should take his assertion a paragraph later that "the events in my life always refuse to happen in normal chronological order, usually occurring backwards." His passivity in the face of uncanny occurrences would support the idea that he truly lived as if all phenomena were absurd. When two of his students hired masked men to kidnap him from the cafeteria of the School of the Art Institute of

Chicago, he went along quietly, thinking, he later claimed, that characters from his films had come to attack him.

His cinema bears witness to "the arbitrariness of all information.' Seldom able to afford more than one roll of film in his early years, he disciplined himself to make the most of a few images. When what came back from the processing labs did not match his original intentions – and it rarely did – he would make a new film around the texture and colors of the footage then at his disposal. He may have been the first important filmmaker to utilize unsplit 8mm film for the two sets of moving images it rendered on 16mm (in *Fleming Faloon*). But when a lab ignored his instructions and sent him back conventional 8mm rolls, he made films out of those too. He was always an original, an isolato.

He began in filmmaking at a time when the psychodramatic, autobiographical mode was dominant, but he wanted to film the most ordinary, least introspective people he could find, often overweight middle-aged men, obsessive television watchers. The central characters of *Fleming Faloon*, *New Improved Institutional Quality: In the Environment of Liquids and Nasals a Parasitic Vowel Sometimes Develops* (1976), and *Wide Angle Saxon* are examples of this type. The paradoxes of representation, not the labyrinth of the self, fascinated him.

The curiosities of religious inspiration can be found even in his first films (e.g., *A Stringent Prediction at the Early Hermaphroditic Stage* [1961]), long before his serial conversions. Landow was raised as a Conservative Jew in a family that observed neither kosher laws nor ritual practices. I recall him taking his bar mitzvah seriously, but a year or two after it, he spoke of himself as a skeptic and an agnostic. Nevertheless, as he wrote years later in the letter to Brakhage, I cited, though he remained a skeptic, his discovery of medieval organum – that first stirring of polyphony in plainchant – had "produced an experience which can be roughly called 'mystical' and 'ecstatic,'" he added, "I read biographies of saints and *The Varieties of Religious Experience* and knew that the experiences I was having were related to those I read about." By the late 1960s, he was flirting with exotic religions: Scientology, Hinduism, and Buddhism. He adapted the title of his film *Bardo Follies* (1967) from *The Tibetan Book of the Dead* and found the title for its successor, *The Film That Rises to the Surface of Clarified Butter* (1968), in the *Upanishads*. His major conversion occurred in the early 1970s. "As a result of a pharmaceutical experience," he confided to Brakhage, he had "a glimpse of the multiplicity of the unseen world." This gave rise to a series of mainstream and esoteric Christian affiliations in waves of enthusiasm and disaffection: Gnosticism, Messianic Judaism, Christian Fundamentalism (and a brief marriage to a scriptural literalist), and, finally, his own fusion of Christianity and Tantra.

His ancestors were Jews from Lithuania in the Russian Empire. When Mekas told him *Landow* sounded like the word for "doghouse" in Lithuanian, he considered translating his name to Farmer Doghouse. He sometimes called himself Apollo Jize or Orphan Morphan. By the late 1980s, though, he consistently went by Owen Land, (the new Lando: The *O* or *Ow* was transposed from Landow and *wen* spelled *new* backward). He had always been addicted to palindromes and anagrams; his titles *Are Era* (1962) and *No Sir, Orison!* (1975) and the palindromes "Malayalam" and "A Man, a Plan, a Canal: Panama!" in *Wide Angle Saxon* are only the most obvious instances.

He denied that his pseudonym encoded his passion for owning land, but I didn't believe him. Not many others knew how often he purchased rundown properties, finagled students to make repairs, and flipped the houses. I heard stories of places he had owned in Bisbee, Arizona, San Francisco, Chicago, New York City, and Tivoli, New York, but he rarely bought more than one at a time. There may well have been others I did not know of: He was particularly secretive about his finances, and his parsimony was legendary. Ben Lazarus, who worked the boom on *Dialogues* but wasn't paid what he'd been promised, took revenge by posting online the pathetic yet hilarious documentary he made about the filmmaker's exploitations and evasions (*In the Land of Owen*, vimeo.com/8053079).

Although Landow's films of the second half of the '60s – from *This Film Will Be Interrupted After 11 Minutes by a Commercial* (1965) to *Institutional Quality* (1969) – were among the earliest, most profound, and most influential instances of what I later identified as "structural film," he never tired of satirizing the idea of that mode of filmmaking or his role in advancing it. He had no scruples about mercilessly making fun of his fellow filmmakers (and of me) so long as he prominently mocked himself in his own works, as he did with wry humor in films such as *New Improved Institutional Quality* and *On the Marriage Broker Joke*. His religious convictions never dispelled his fascination with the absurdities of human behavior. The drives for possessions, certitude, beauty, sex, money, and food – especially sex – make Land's fictive humans ridiculous, confused, and devious. His ability to invent and to people his films with memorably ridiculous characters was unmatched, even by the late George Kuchar, among American avant-garde filmmakers.

Mekas, as I wrote above, was the first to recognize the genius of Landow, but Marjorie Keller was the first to appreciate the greatness of Saul Levine as a filmmaker. He has been one of the most underrated in the American avant-garde cinema throughout his more than fifty-year-long career. His one-man program at the New York Film Festival in 2006 was his first, although he had been included in group screenings there and elsewhere before. The five films selected for his 2006 show were so old (made between 1967 and 1983) that they were promoted as restored artifacts. Yet if someone were to write a critical history of the avant-garde cinema in Boston (as David James did for Los Angeles in his 2005 book, *The Most Typical Avant-Garde: History and Geography of Minor Cinemas in Los Angeles*), Levine would be its hero. He seldom leaves the city, where, as a professor at the Massachusetts College of Art (dismissed in 2022 on bogus charges), he had been one of the most influential teachers of filmmaking in the nation, and his energies sustained for decades the larger community of avant-garde filmmakers in Boston.

The chief reason for his neglect, or isolation, may not have been his geographical location, however, but his situation was exacerbated by his rather his long commitment to 8mm and Super 8mm formats (although he has blown copies up to 16mm for distribution by the Film-Makers' Cooperative and Canyon Cinema since the 1970s). A figure of the perennial Left, Levine has identified with and championed the small gauges as if they were marginalized citizens of the republic of cinema. By example, he has taught his students to cling to their artistic freedom by seeking out the least expensive modes of filmmaking and, as Emerson wrote in the essay "Experience," to "hold hard to this poverty, however scandalous, and by more vigorous self-recoveries, after the sallies of action, possess our axis more firmly." As a consequence of this ascetic attitude toward the medium, Levine embraced video much earlier than did those of his fellow filmmakers who shared his passion for the texture of celluloid. For instance, Stan Brakhage – with whom Levine studied in the early '70s and who was, more significantly, the greatest influence on his work – resorted to painting on film in his last years rather than make the switch. When the expenses of 16mm production temporarily drove Brakhage into a detour of making first 8mm films (in 1964) and later Super 8mm films (in 1976), he thought of his engagement with the smaller gauges as exemplary for younger filmmakers. Of those who followed his example, Levine has been the most persistent. He started shooting 8mm in 1965, with *Salt of the Sea*, and to this day remains faithful to the small gauge (which he usually converts to video),

Viewing a large span of Levine's work in a short time reveals the grand scale of the project lurking within the humble titles and modest formal ambitions of his insistent efflux of lyrical films. In a sense, to use the terminology of William Butler Yeats, perhaps the foundational poet for this filmmaker who once imagined that poetry would be his vocation, Levine's work might be seen as the *antithetical* counterpart to that of Jonas Mekas. They both give us a vivid feeling for daily life lived in urban America over the past sixty years (add at least ten more for Mekas's oeuvre); few other major avant-garde filmmakers are as convincing at disclosing a world filled with other people as Mekas and Levine (the tragically short-lived Warren Sonbert was of that select company). But whereas Mekas, an irrepressible vitalist, depicts his ambit as a perpetual celebration, an ongoing party attended by art-world and other celebrities, Levine continually probes the margins of the gritty surroundings in which he lives and works for flashes of illumination, purchased at the high cost of a skepticism that seldom permits him either the ecstatic self-exhibition that characterizes Mekas's on-screen moments or the melancholy of Mekas's quite moving voiceover interventions. Surprisingly for a filmmaker so taken with Yeats and so influenced by Brakhage, Levine shows no tolerance for mythopoeia.

Beginning in 1967, with roughly a dozen short films under his belt, Levine spent six years reediting 8mm prints of the Chaplin shorts *Easy Street* (1917) and *In the Park* (1915), incorporating as well television images of an antiwar protests in which the Boston filmmaker participated. The result was *The Big Stick/ An Old Reel* (1967–73), his self-tutorial in montage, the ascesis of narrative, and the beauties of caustic rhythms. In the early stages of that work's construction, Levine was teaching filmmaking at Tufts University, in Medford, Massachusetts, but he would soon be fired, if not specifically for his role in occupying a campus building during a protest over the dismissal of an African-American secretary, then for his political activism generally. Together with (my future wife) filmmaker Marjorie Keller, then a student forced to withdraw from Tufts over the same protest, Levine moved to Chicago to attend graduate school and to edit the national SDS newspaper, *New Left Notes*. A dual portrait of Keller and himself amid rounds of political protests is at the heart of Levine's most impressive early film, *New Left Note* (1968–82). Its title conjoins the SDS publication with his still ongoing series of films, all called "Notes," which may well be his central achievement as a filmmaker. (He had made thirteen films in this series by 2007].) The deceptively modest term identifies the primary conceit of these films – that they are epistolary gestures, made to convey the news of what is happening in the filmmaker's life – while suggesting that they are also unitary points in an extended melody. The rapid montage of *New Left Note* effectively levels and integrates the welter of events and perceptions amassed in the film: Nixon on television, thousands gathered on the New Haven Green to support Bobby Seale, friends soaking in a public fountain, street marches against the war in Vietnam, and luminous glimpses of the filmmaker's domestic life with Keller, his new girlfriend at that time.

New Left Note was an early intimation of the persistent emphasis on companionship that would become a hallmark of Levine's cinema. In the video works of the recent past, we can see clearly the remarkable capacity and talent for friendship that has been a primary source of his artistic strength since he began to make films. In his ongoing series "Driven," begun in 2002, Levine rides in the front seat of an automobile while one of his friends talks about his or her life for eighty-two minutes (the maximum length of a single take using his digital camera). The initial ten installments he has made unwittingly disclose the generosity of the filmmaker. He is often quiet, patient with the occasional long pauses when his driver falls silent, yet he is willing to talk about himself when questioned, as he is by filmmaker Asma Kazmi in the 2005 episode he made with her. By having his subjects drive him around the city at night, he disengages much of the self-consciousness inherent in the interview genre. Because of the choice of his subjects, or perhaps by the sheer dint of his own antinomian personality, the monologues inevitably turn to narratives of resistance to institutions, laws, family pressures. Levine's low-key mode of inquiry and his genuine passion for listening have an infectious power. Sometimes his driver makes it easy for him: The filmmaker Joe Gibbons, to whom he devoted two installments in 2002, is an ironic raconteur who does not require Levine's skillful intervention to fascinate us for almost an hour and a half at a stretch. What is remarkable is how engaging the filmmaker manages to make his less flamboyant interlocutors.

The "Driven" series illuminates the sometimes-elusive persona at the heart of Levine's finest films. They intimate his acceptance of, almost resignation to, isolation, which gives a melancholy, elegiac air to many of the early films; yet at the same time they reveal his hungry curiosity about the lives and feelings of others and his democratic joy of being in company. In a retrospective light, we can see the "Notes" as gestures toward absent friends, sometimes unnamed, whose very absence inspires him to weigh the events of his daily life. The exquisite, brief, lyric *Crescent* (1993) is paradigmatic of Levine's mature art. With a handheld camera, the filmmaker pans several times, over the course of three or four shots, between the sliver of a moon at sunset and distant lights. By the last of these shots, night has come. On the soundtrack we hear Levine's conversation with filmmaker Pelle Lowe, who tells him the story of an umbrella her father had made for her mother. When Lowe asks Levine if his parents also told stories of their youth as they grew older, he says no – they told their stories when they were younger; in old age they fell silent. The dialogue is utterly natural, beautifully timed, as if it were spontaneously occurring as Lowe and Levine sat observing the moon and the night lights. Lowe, like many of the subjects of "Driven," was a student of Levine's, whom he encouraged, nurtured, and promoted, although I suspect he would resist that description of their relationship: He is so thoroughly a democrat that he acts as if he merely provides the already formed filmmakers in his classes with equipment, shows them films he admires, and makes a few observations about their work.

The poetic strength of *Crescent* derives from the tensions between the images and the soundtrack. Image alone never carries Levine films. His silent films depend upon editing so fast and insistent that the tiny 8mm frame is nearly overwhelmed with the labored cutting and gluing. The montage of his *Note to Colleen* (1974) programmatically devalues imagery *per se*, juxtaposing people and portraits, natural objects and painted images, at what may be the Washington Square Art Fair in New York. The film asserts that filmmaking, at least as Levine practices it, is a relational, more than a representational art. Here and elsewhere, he makes capital of his limitations as a cinematographer (apparently related to his poor eyesight). The title of the portrait *Portrayal/ Near Site* (1977–78) calls attention to his nearsightedness, but Levine compensates by filming a young woman extremely close up, as they make love on the grass. At its most compelling, Levine's photography conveys an erotic intensity, especially in capturing intimate moments with women: thus, the shots of Keller stand out in *New Left Note*, and whole films such as *Note to Poli* (1982–83) and *Portrayal/ Sheryl Kaye* (1977) indicate the visionary power of sexuality for the filmmaker.

In *Whole Note* (2000–2001), he achieves an equally loving intensity by fixing his camera on his father in the last days of his life. But Levine can also generate a successful film from a mere nothing, as when he examines a black-and-white photograph of the young Picasso clipped from a magazine and taped to a windowpane in *Shmateh III* (1983–84). The series title borrows the Yiddish word for "rag," to underscore the throwaway status of the image source. Yet another, later series, "Light Licks" (1999–), sidesteps the problems of imagery by generating almost musical rhythmic structures abstracted from colored light sources.

The critical turning point in Levine's early career came when he acquired a Super 8mm sound camera in 1976, just as he was losing his job teaching filmmaking at SUNY, Binghamton (again his political activism got him in trouble). Thus, the title of *Notes of an Early Fall* (1976) refers to the season in which he returns to his family home with his new camera to celebrate Rosh Hashanah, as well as to the aesthetic fall from the grace of pure vision into the worldly cacophony of synchronous sound (in a hyperbole of Brakhage's polemics) and the fall from a prestigious position in what was at the time the strongest academic program in avant-garde filmmaking in America. For most of the film's thirty-three minutes, the filmmaker turned his back on his earlier montage style; instead, he fixed his camera on images of repetition: he shot a phonographic record so warped the needle flew randomly within a range of three or four grooves for nearly two hundred cycles; then he filmed a small bird trying to pass through a closed window over and over again, children playing in a park, and animals pacing in cages in a zoo. Late in the film he brought these elements together through montage and intercut them with a portrait of his family on the eve of the Jewish New Year's holiday. There is a brief image of President Carter on television, speaking of our misused resources as if he were telling the nation of the filmmaker's predicament.

Levine wrote in response to my inquiry about the warped disk:

> The record is by Champion Jack Dupree, a New Orleans pianist and blues player who often did 'talking' blues. The LP is called *Tricks*, from a talking blues entitled 'Tricks Don't Walk No More,' a whore's lament about the change in work with the advent of automobiles. On the record we're mainly hearing a cut about his dog not recognizing him when he comes home from a long road trip, since his wife has another lover. The song also refers to racism and him getting beaten up by the police. He's very funny in a dark way. He lived mainly in Paris to escape from a society he saw as white supremacist.

Levine himself is "funny in a dark way" in this crucial film and in its companion piece, *Departure* (1976–84), which depicts the anxieties of his friends and colleagues at Binghamton as they anticipate leaving the university environment. In that film, he combines talking interviews with montage, directly cutting across, and thereby disrupting, the sound of the single-system Super 8mm, violating the implicit rules of synchronization. (On a conventional filmstrip the sound runs more than a second ahead of the image to allow for the threading of the projector. Typically, sound and picture are edited on two independent tracks and then "married" in a final print. Single-system sound cameras were designed for home movies, with no provision for editing. Levine's staccato editing method capitalized on that negative provision.)

Whereas insistent repetition was an expression of frustration and blues in *Notes of an Early Fall*, it would become a focus of exuberant playfulness in the second of Levine's *Raps and Chants* (1981–82). There, filmmaker Caroline Avery sits for her film portrait, thoroughly amusing herself, and presumably Levine, by hitting the buttons on a tape recorder to improvise a sound composition out of fragments of music and protest chants. As if responding to the rhythms of Avery's pizzicato, Levine sometimes records images so rapidly that he obliterates the sound for a few seconds. The calculus of silence and sound, art and song, eros and time, at stake in this film, and in his major work of the early '80s, reflects a favorite poem of Levine's, "After Long Silence," in which Yeats wrote:

> Speech after long silence; it is right,
> All other lovers being estranged or dead,
> Unfriendly lamplight hid under its shade,
> The curtains drawn upon unfriendly night,
> That we descant and yet again descant
> Upon the supreme theme of Art and Song:
> Bodily decrepitude is wisdom; young
> We loved each other and were ignorant.

His *Notes After Long Silence* (1984–89) takes its title from Yeats's poem and fuses an encounter with Levine's former wife and her two children from a subsequent marriage with images of sex, construction work, the war in Vietnam, and B. B. King singing on television. Here, Levine's version of the "supreme theme of Art and Song" recalls that of Brakhage and especially of Brakhage's longest 8mm film, *23rd Psalm Branch* (1966–67), in which he struggled to raise the pain and confusion of his response to the Vietnam War to the cinematic equivalent of silent song. In deviating from Brakhage's mode by utilizing fragmentary synchronized sound, Levine crafted his own version of the crisis film, in which the labor of filmmaking continually constructs and mourns a world on the verge of dissolution. But he resists Brakhage's drive toward resolution, as if a synthetic or culminating moment were a fiction that failed to console him. Instead, montage becomes a form of insistence, a coefficient of the political pressure that must be ceaselessly renewed in the face of entropy. That seems to be the wisdom of the three-part series composed of *A Few Tunes Going Out: Bopping the Great Wall of China Blue* (1978–79), *Groove to Groove* (1978–82), and *A Brennen Soll Columbus N Medina* (1978–84). The first focused on his friend the filmmaker, Dan Barnett (who left his position at SUNY, Binghamton, at the same time as Levine), as he assists a woman with the editing of her thesis film; the second, on radio DJ Mai Cramer and Levine himself at his editing table; and the last, on patriotic songs, centrally those recalled by the filmmaker's mother and aunts while Ray Charles sings "America the Beautiful" on TV. These films underscore the uniqueness of the auditory environment of Levine's cinema: a world of broken syllables, Yiddish jokes, nearly forgotten songs, phrases and music seeping out of the omnipresent television. His films assert the imperative to reconnect shattered sounds and pictures into a speech that does not disguise their cacophony.

Landow and Levine were contemporaries. They grew up with televisions in their homes, as the earlier generation of Brakhage, Anger, Markopoulos, Deren, *et al.* did not. In Levine's films politics occupies a central role, as religion and language do for Landow.

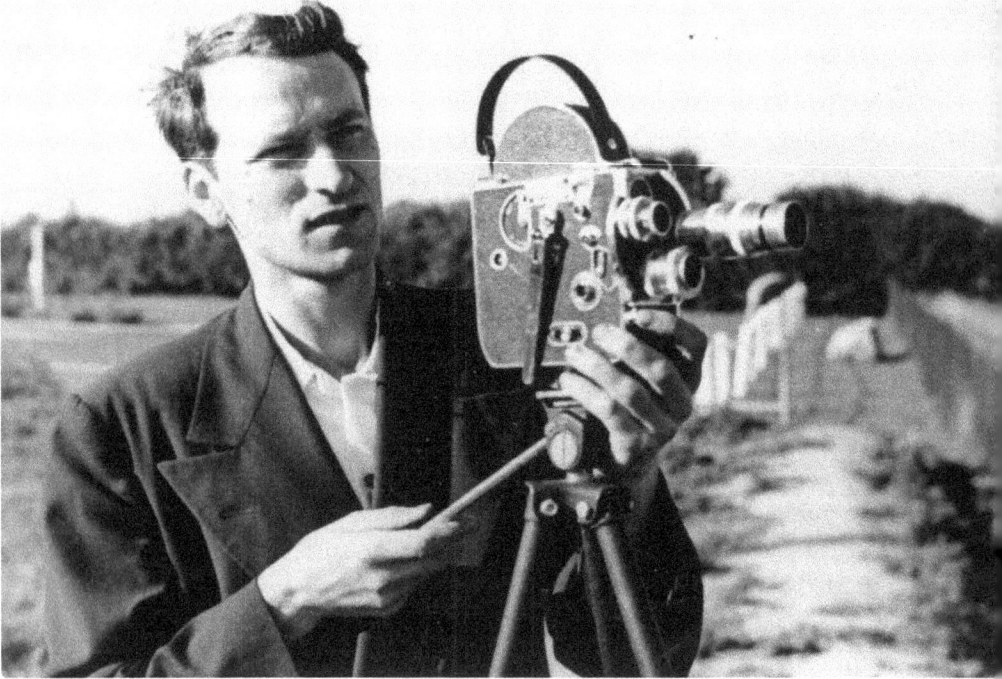

Jonas Mekas, 1950
(courtesy Spector Books).

Marjorie Keller.

George Landow.

Saul Levine.

Stanley Cavell
and
Ken Kelman

In this final Pairing, I shall consider two theorists of cinema who postulated the Realism as the essence of the medium from very different perspectives. One of them, Stanley Cavell, was internationally renowned, the other, Ken Kelman, was virtually unknown. I am familiar with Cavell only from his writings; Kelman was a personal friend for many years. I may be one of the few living persons who first heard of Stanley Cavell as a character in an avant-garde film, David Brooks's *The Wind Is Driving him Toward the Open Sea* (1968) where he appears among a trio of philosophers along with Columbia University's Arthur Danto and Sidney Morgenbesser.

I read his *The World Viewed* as soon as it was published in 1971. Although I was outraged (and even at times disgusted) by that first reading, I was touched by its eloquence; for he and Kelman were both distinguished prose stylists. My hostility was undoubtedly the premature judgment of a champion of avant-garde cinema toward a thinker whose taste differed so radically from mine. I could hardly attend to what Cavell actually wrote at that time. My rage began with the opening chapter's claim that "...in the case of films, it is generally true that you do not really like the highest instances unless you also like the typical ones."

[TWV, 6] Here, I thought, was a parodic example of a professorial movie buff, taking what the Brattle Cinema in Cambridge happened to screen as it were the art of film. Yet in that very book he amply suggests that only a fool would judge paintings or music on the same basis. The fifteenth of *The World Viewed*'s nineteen chapters, called "Excursus: Some Modernist Painting," drove home to me what a loss Cavell's mind and pen were to what I then considered serious film study. In that chapter he brilliantly enacted the characteristic moves of his best writing; above all, by investing aesthetic distinctions with moral values. It didn't take the copious footnotes to show how indebted his choice of privileged paintings was to Michael Fried's controversial (and dubious) taste. Yet his way of writing about them was astounding, and very moving:

> Acceptance of such objects achieves the absolute acceptance of the moment, by defeating the sway of the momentous. It is an ambition worthy of the highest art. Nothing is of greater moment than the knowledge that the choice of one moment excludes another, that no moment makes up for another, that the significance of one moment is the cost of what it forgoes. That is refinement. Beauty and significance, except in youth, are born of loss. But otherwise everything is lost. The last knowledge will be to allow even that knowledge of loss to vanish, to see whether the world regains. The idea of infinite possibility is the pain, and the balm, of adolescence. The only return on becoming adult, the only justice in forgoing that world of possibility, is the reception of actuality – the pain and balm in the truth of the only world: that it exists, and I in it.

I had never read such Emersonian eloquence in defense of – in the description of the experience of – abstract painting. Sure: I had known that Cavell was a figure of the Harvard Philosophy Department who was beginning to bridge the abyss that then separated the readers of Anglo-American post-Wittgenstein analysis from the work of Heidegger. In the 'Excursus" to *The World Viewed* one could see that bridgework in operation, as Cavell pitted the 'moment' against the 'momentous' in the passage above, and even more brilliantly in his extensions of the words of "automatism," "candid," "medium," "representation" and "abstract" in that same chapter. Consider how he marshalled asyndeton to spin out the 'abstract' nouns for the psychological and moral distractions such paintings obliterated, and then capped the observation poignantly with a verbless riff of near rhyme:

> Because these abstractions retain the power of art, after the failure of representations to depict our conviction and connectedness with the world, they have overcome the representativeness which came between our reality and our art: overcame it by abstraction, abstracting us from *the recognitions and engagements and complicities and privileged appeals and protests* which distracted us from one another and from the world we have constructed. *Attracted from distraction by abstraction."* (TWV, 117, my italics)

His diction echoes and twists key terms previously used in the chapter. Earlier he had boldly conflated representation as *mimesis* with political representation [*praesens*] without the slightest Heideggerian pretense to philological authority or to the recovery of an ancient synthesis. The paintings alone were sufficient authority, and the language of the philosopher *represented* the depth of his response to them.

Luckily, the intensity and acuity of his moral vision of art impelled me to acquire *Must We Mean What We Say?* as soon as I could afford it. I write "Luckily" – because otherwise I might never have found a reason to read his essay "Kierkegaard's *On Authority and Religion.*" That essay allowed me to complete the dissertation I was struggling to write on Maurice Blanchot and Charles Olson. At that time, the scholarship and writing on Blanchot was scarce and thin. Most of what there was was French, and none of its authors seemed interested in tracing Blanchot's references. I had been able to pick out of his early writings unattributed phrases that he culled from Hegel, the Latin Vulgate, Heine, Ponge, and Kierkegaard, but it wasn't until I read Cavell's essay that I knew what I might do with that arcana. Cavell had read Kierkegaard on authority as a proleptic text on modern art (among many other things, of less pertinence to me). Suddenly in the light reflected from Cavell's pages I saw all those oblique quotations of Blanchot's as attempts to define the impossible task of writing and representation in literature. That made my mundane task of academic writing possible.

Without meticulous biographies it would be impossible to untangle the priorities in the Cavell/ Fried relationship. Fried probably would not have known Cavell's Kierkegaard essay when he published "Art and Objecthood" in 1967. (Cavell might not have even written it by then: it appeared in his 1969 collection of essays.) By opening "Art and Objecthood" with a quotation from Perry Miller, (the Harvard historian of Puritan theology) and ending with the dictum, "Presentness is grace," Fried eventually earned the contempt of such colleagues as Rosalind Krauss and Hal Foster for his capitulation to the language of religion, while I found that hint of the metamorphosis of Puritan theology to the theory of art the most fascinating aspect of his polemic. But the explicit claims of Cavell were nevertheless more illuminating, as when he writes

> ...our serious art is produced under conditions which Kierkegaard announces as those of apostleship, not those of genius. I do not insist that art has become religion (which may or may not describe the situation...) but that the activity of modern art, both in production and reception, is to be understood in categories which are, or were, religious. (MWMWWS, 175)

Between *The World Viewed* and *Pursuits of Happiness* he wrote *Senses of Walden*. I could not understand why Cavell was focusing his attention on Thoreau and ignoring Emerson, the primary poet-philosopher of America. Of course, I did not realize then that I was repeating my previous error of judging the book by its ostensible critical subject. It took *Pursuits of Happiness*, a book utterly outside of my academic domain and territorial interests, to make me an avid reader of all that Cavell wrote.

At the time that I was reading *The Senses of Walden*, one of my preoccupations was the Americanness of the American avant-garde cinema. Because I was so obsessed with the tropes filmmakers had forged from walking with a movie camera, or turning it upside down, or filming from cars, trains, and airplanes, a hitherto overlooked passage in the "Idealism" section of Emerson's 1836 book *Nature* drew my attention (as cited on p. pp. 149-150).

Consequently, a statement by Tony Smith, disparaged by Fried in "Art and Objecthood" where I first encountered it, thrilled me:

> When I was teaching at Cooper Union in the first year or two of the '50s, someone told me how I could get on to the unfinished New Jersey Turnpike. I took three students and drove from somewhere in the Meadows to New Brunswick. It was a dark night and there were no lights or shoulder markers, lines, railings or anything at all except the dark pavement moving through the landscape of the flats, rimmed by hills in the distance, but punctuated by stacks, towers, fumes and colored lights. This drive was a revealing experience. The road and much of the landscape was artificial, and yet it couldn't be called a work of art. On the other hand, it did something for me that art had never done. At first I didn't know what it was, but its effect was to liberate me from many of the views I had had about art. It seemed that there had been a reality there which had not had any expression in art.

The aesthetic results of these 'experiences' are positively manifested in avant-garde cinema and polemically misapplied to sculpture and painting by Fried. One of my mistakes was thinking then that Cavell's closeness to Fried and his insistence on the artistic priority of Hollywood films, and their escape from the demands of Modernism, blinded him to this, and generally to the aesthetic dimensions of Emerson's philosophy. But when he turned, eventually, to Emerson, he revealed profundities in the bard of Concord that I hadn't been able to see.

Every few years in my long tenure at Princeton University I would offer a course in Film Theory. *The World Viewed* was usually included on the syllabus, making me fonder of it with each iteration. One time, co-teaching the course with Thomas Levin, a delightfully good-natured agonist whose perpetual disagreements with me enlivened such collaboration, I saw, as in a funhouse mirror, my own earlier prejudices toward Cavell incarnated by my colleague, who also deplored the objects valued in that book, but not for the same reasons I had discounted it. It was great fun to become, at last, Cavell's advocate, and illuminating to reveal to myself the utter irrelevance of the cinematic objects of discussion.

By then I had met Cavell a few times. His generosity and kindness were outstanding. Over time the logic of his inquiries brought him to accept and champion what had been my own youthful enthusiasms, Emerson and Heidegger – and in so doing he gave us very useful instruction in what was most valuable in them – although he never "acknowledged' the importance of avant-garde cinema. Now that "film," as we both knew it, is a matter of the past and Modernism is no longer an arena of high stakes contention, the grounds of what had been our ideological opposition have dissolved into the atmosphere of critical history where my dispute will be an irrelevant footnote to his permanent eminence.

Ken Kelman died in late spring 2017 a year before Cavell. At the time he was still writing plays, but he probably had not written about cinema for at least ten years. In fact, as far as I know, the only new film he had seen in the twenty-first century was Jerome Hiler's *Words of Mercury* (2011) at the Whitney Museum of American Art in March 2012. I know that only because I urged him to attend the screening with me. It was the last time I saw him, although we spoke on the telephone a few times after that.

Kelman was a hoarder. His apartment was overflowing with Tibetan art, manuscripts of his plays and unpublished novels, lots of prose, perhaps recordings of his lectures, and probably even gold coins. He was a tireless advocate for collecting gold, assured that the paper money economy was about to collapse.

We met in 1959 or 1960 in New Haven, when I was attending high school, and he was at the Yale Drama School studying playwriting under John Gassner. I had founded the New Haven Film Society in order to see classic films, mostly silent. In that period before videotapes, cassettes, or DVDs it was nearly impossible to see such films outside of New York City (and even there it was supremely difficult). The Yale Film Society hosted weekly screenings that showed old films, but never silent ones. They hardly deviated from what was then the dominant taste of students: every year they showed *Casablanca* and *From Here to Eternity*.

Kelman was a regular patron of the New Haven Film Society where every week standard film classics, such as *The Battleship Potemkin* and *The Cabinet of Dr. Caligari* were screened. He stood out, perpetually wearing a dark trench coat, walking with the slightest stoop, apparently oblivious to everything around him. When I encountered him on the streets near the university, I always walked and talked with him. There was no way to get in touch otherwise. At first, I assumed he was gay because he always came to the film society screenings accompanied by a male painter from the Yale Art School. I was wrong. Kelman was a heterosexual, celibate as long as I knew him except for two very brief affairs with young women. Before enrolling at the Yale Drama School, he had been at Harvard Law School – from which he dropped out – and in the army – from which he was given a general discharge as "untrainable."

He knew more about cinema than anyone I had met until that time. He told me about the work of Robert Bresson and Carl Dreyer's sound films. (I had already made a trip to New York to see Dreyer's silent *La passion de Jeanne d'Arc* when the New Yorker Theater gave a rare, one-night screening of it.) He taught me to appreciate Alfred Hitchcock's *Vertigo* and the charisma of Louise Brooks, although I could never share his later enthusiasm for such soft-core cult films as *Olga's House of Shame* (1964). In turn, I persuaded him of the glories of the American avant-garde cinema.

Kelman wrote very quickly and beautifully. At the New Haven Film Society, I had started a mimeographed journal, *Filmwise*. It grew out of the notes we handed to the audience before screenings. The first issue as a full-fledged journal was completely devoted to the work of Stan Brakhage. After that, each issue was centered on one or two filmmakers: Maya Deren, Gregory Markopoulos, Willard Maas and Marie Menken. I asked Kelman if he would write something on Deren's *Ritual in Transfigured Time* (1946) for the second issue. After watching the film a half-dozen or so times, he quickly wrote a brilliant essay, "Widow into Bride." He obliged again for the Maas/ Menken issue (our last).

In the fall of 1963, I took a leave from college to prepare the first International Exposition of the New American Cinema to tour European cities. I was living in New York, assisting Jonas Mekas in editing *Film Culture*. Kelman attended screenings with me several days each week, writing pieces on many films for the magazine. His remarkable insights and lightning writing speed were great assets to us. Just one day after the first screenings of Markopoulos's *Twice a Man*, Jack Smith's *Flaming Creatures*, and Kenneth Anger's *Scorpio Rising*, Kelman delivered finished texts on each of them to the *Film Culture* office. He also wrote most of the accolades for the *Film Culture* annual awards in the late Sixties and early Seventies.

He was wonderfully articulate – but weird. In New Haven, if I wanted to stop in a luncheonette for coffee or a burger, he would eat or drink nothing. He said he was trying to live on an exclusive diet of Kellogg's Special K cereal, so that after leaving the Drama School he could live cheaply in New York City without working or working only minimally. In actuality, he moved into his parents' apartment, and died there some fifty years later. The only regular job I knew him to have taken was a year teaching film history at Bard College in the early Seventies, replacing me after I resigned.

Kelman was notoriously frugal, a comical skinflint. To get him to accept invitations to dinner in my home, I had to provide him with two bus tokens for his trips crosstown from his parents' apartment on East Eighty-Third Street to mine, then on West Eighty-Eighth. At the same time, he was stupendously generous. If one asked to borrow thousands of dollars from him, he would groan first, then bring the cash the next day. He never asked for a receipt. Nor did he mention the loan – sometimes for years – before it was repaid. I suspect several such debts were still outstanding when he died.

When he did come to dinner at my house, or that of the architect Raimund Abraham, or less frequently at Jonas Mekas's loft, he carried an astonishing array of pills that he swallowed before eating. He would never eat anything hot, just as he would never touch a person, even to shake hands. His familiarity with changing health-regimen fads was impressive; he subscribed to several. When Daniel Pinkwater (to whom I introduced Kelman fifty years ago: they became fast friends) informed me of his death, he attributed it to malnutrition. Apparently, Kelman believed his intake of pills was all he needed.

He saw films at the Museum of Modern Art, the Film-Makers' Cinematheque, and at private screenings when he was invited, but rarely, if ever, in conventional theaters, where he would have had to purchase a ticket. He did watch old movies on television, but only when they followed a basketball game. That was his preferred sport, although he loved games and puzzles of all sorts. To play Scrabble with him would have been a massive humiliation if it were not so amusing to see how he accumulated astronomical scores, using up all of his letters several times in each game and rarely failing to place a q or an x on the triple-score square. The only time I ever saw him display intense emotion was when he was furious over what he took to be a violation of the rules of Monopoly.

He did crossword puzzles faster than I could write, bragging that he could do the Sunday New York Times crossword entirely between any two stops on the Lexington IRT subway. He even splurged to enter a national crossword puzzle contest, falsely convinced he would win the big financial prize, only to be frustrated when he learned that he alone of the top twenty contestants wasn't a professional crossword editor or author. Soon after I met him, he had been just as sure he would win a fortune from the "Famous Faces" contest in one of the New York tabloid newspapers. He was forever entering such competitions, never winning them.

All his adult life Kelman was primarily a dramatist. After he left the Yale Drama School, he would write a play a year; longhand first, then transposed to his typewriter. In his later years he wrote plays less frequently. His enthusiasm for his most recent work was always unbounded. I believe he was convinced he was the greatest living playwright. In 1968, the year of his lecture series "Exercises in Film History" at the Film-Makers' Cinematheque on 80 Wooster Street, he also acted in the first of Richard Foreman's Ontological-Hysteric Theater productions, *Angelface*. Foreman, who had been at the Yale Drama School with Kelman, also used the Film-Makers' Cinematheque space to launch his theater. He was the only American contemporary in the theater I ever heard Kelman praise.

In later years, Kelman believed his fantasy of a Broadway production was within reach: his father had left a couple of rundown apartment buildings on Long Island to him and his sister, who was a few years younger; she was negotiating their sale the last time he and I spoke, some months before his sudden death. With his share of the sale, he planned to mount a production of his play 'Four Sisters' on Broadway. He was not concerned that it might close after a night or two: for him, the expense of two or three million dollars would be worth it.

Over the years, I have often received inquiries from people who did not know Kelman, asking why he was on the selection committee of the "Essential Cinema" for Anthology Film Archives when it began in 1970. Although he had ceased going to films and wrote nothing about cinema in the decades prior to his death, in 1968 he was still a prominent figure at the Film-Makers' Cinematheque. Mekas, its director, had asked him to give a series of lectures on the history of cinema. They agreed upon a full year's sequence – fifty-two Thursday night screenings followed by an analytical and historical lecture every Monday evening, to be entitled "Exercises in Film History." Consequently, when the selection committee for Anthology Film Archives was formed two years later, Kelman was the best informed and most articulate film historian of the group. Already, at that time, he identified himself as an "ex–film critic."

The scope of his knowledge of cinema and the depth of his insight were astounding. He was the most articulate and least polemical member of the "Essential Cinema" selection committee. After fifty years, I have come to realize that he was almost always right about his inclusions and exclusions. The selection process for the "Essential Cinema" collection had been conceived as ongoing and perpetual. But a severe financial crisis in 1972 ended it. The theater had to move from its initial location in Joseph Papp's Public Theater on Lafayette Street, first to 80 Wooster Street, the home of the former Film-Makers' Cinematheque, and, many years later, to its current location, a former courthouse at Second Avenue and Second Street. Likewise, the published anthology of essays about the collection, *The Essential Cinema*, was intended to be issued annually. That too had to be terminated when the promised funding was withdrawn. It was no accident that the essays by Kelman dominated the initial volume; he wrote on Erich von Stroheim's *Greed* (1924); Luis Buñuel's first three films; all four of Jean Vigo's films; Leni Riefenstahl's *The Triumph of the Will*; Robert Bresson's *Pickpocket* (1959); Helen Levitt, Janice Loeb, and James Agee's *In the Street* (1948); Stan Brakhage's *Anticipation of the Night*; and Bruce Conner's *Report* (1967). Those filmmakers, and most of those films, were among those screened (or scheduled to be screened) in Kelman's earlier "Exercises in Film History."

Kelman always lectured without a prepared text, depending

on a fresh screening of the film to inspire his ideas. He was brutally honest about his ignorance of foreign languages, and repeatedly acknowledged aspects of the films he did not comprehend. Yet he was convinced that in the act of discussing them he would discover their fundamental coherences. Thus, questions from the audience about specific images elicited new interpretations as often as confessions of bafflement. In lecturing he exhibited acts of discovery and demonstrated the workings of his acute sensibility, such as his ability to situate all the films he showed in a historical tradition. He distinguished covert influences and formal allegiances between films with great conviction. Both before and after "Exercises in Film History," he wrote important synoptic aesthetic speculations on the history of cinema: "Classic Plastics and Total Tectonics" and "Cinema as Poetry" were among the most important of these in the early period; and "Animal Cinema" and the lecture, "Megafilm and Metafilm," afterwards. Perhaps even more startling was his ability to convincingly articulate the bases of the links he saw between very different films. Who but Kelman would have noticed the affinity of Peter Kubelka's *Mosaik im Vertrauen* with Walter Ruttmann's *Berlin*? Or Isidore Isou's *Traité de bave et d'éternité* with Jean Cocteau's *Le sang d'un poète*?

An evolving theory of the essence of cinema subtends all of Kelman's speculations on film history. Its most sophisticated articulation can be found in "Animal Cinema," perhaps his last writing on film. In it, Kelman writes that the static images of the individual frames – often of people no longer living – are "raised from the dead" by the rapidly flickering light of the projector. The concept of "Life" resonates throughout his writings on film.

I do not know if he ever read all the way through Siegfried Kracauer's *A Theory of Film* (1960); Cavell surely did and found it a significant inspiration, although he evidentially preferred Bazin's formalism to Kracauer's sociology. I am convinced Kelman perused Kracauer's book, at least. To a remarkable degree, he shared its thesis that the primary function of cinema has been to represent reality. In this respect, Kracauer leaned heavily on Georg Simmel's Lebensphilosophie. I am equally convinced that Kelman knew nothing of Simmel. He didn't read philosophy, as far as I could tell. In fact, I believe he did most of his serious reading before I had met him. Herman Melville and Georg Büchner remained his primary literary touchstones for his whole life. He knew Greek tragedy and Shakespeare thoroughly, and I recall him extolling Leo Tolstoy as a dramatist.

Apparently, Kelman came by his affinity with Kracauer from his intense scrutiny of most of the same films that the German-American social theorist studied, rather than being stimulated by Kracauer's own insights. Yet the differences of their orientations are more significant than their overlappings. Kelman's passion for cinema was tied to his antirational and pessimistic, or rather tragic, view of existence. The realism he continually noted in the essence of cinema was always "magical." Life revealed itself in its illusions. Eschewing the sociological perspective that made Kracauer apprehensive of *The Cabinet of Dr. Caligari* and horrified by *The Triumph of the Will*, Kelman praised the former as a masterpiece of cinematic subjectivity, and the latter as the cinema's ultimate "transfiguration" of matter into spirit. The specter of death is explicit in the former, and implicit, but even more palpable, in the latter through the historical fate it helped set in motion.

Kelman came to cinema with the tragic conviction that Life is most vivid (or, in his terms, "intense") in the face of Death. A year or so before embarking on "Exercises in Film History," he sent a letter to Louise Brooks, seeking material for a novel he had started writing, to be called *The Autobiography of Death: Fantasia on Louise Brooks* or *Meditation on Louis Brooks*. In that letter he confessed that after re-watching one of her silent films, "the beauties of the past deluged me. I was obsessed with time, mortality, change."

After the 1989 production of his play "Dead Still," he composed an (unpublished) polemical abecedarium about his theater. Under "L" we find:

> LIFE 1: I do not practice animation art. The so-called life (characters) of most drama is cartoons. No matter how lifelike, complex, humanly interesting, they are precisely animated. If someone on the stage just yells at us, we react with utmost intensity. It is certainly felt as life, though we know nothing of the shouter's internal process. Why must we be aware of all the machinery at work? Is it so exquisite? So credible? The shout is crude life, it lacks the complexity and elaboration possible in a nicely detailed cartoon. I prefer it, not on the grounds of verisimilitude but of veracity.
> LIFE 2: The wages of life is death. The price is right.

The bias toward realism in the "Exercises in Film History" and in his other writings and lectures on film is merely apparent and superficial. Kelman always extolled the cinema for its ways of representing Life. The innovations in technique and perspective that he repeatedly made the center of his arguments were always methods of intensifying the Life he recognized in the films he discussed, fantasies as well as documentaries, avant-garde film poems as well as naturalist narratives. Even when he erred in his interpretation, his keen observation of the dimensions of Life the filmmaker sought to capture made his analyses invaluable. The Life Kelman found in great cinema was a matter of the infusion of Spirit into the dead material of film frames. He charted the variations on Spirit as they manifested in the films he loved: as breath, wind, inspiration. Yahweh, Frankenstein, and Jesus were central emblems of the filmmaker for him.

Yet he subscribed to no religion. His family was Jewish, but not practicing. Once he told me he was not even circumcised, and that his father wasn't either. When I asked how this came about, since it was virtually unheard of among Jews of his generation not to circumcise boys, he told me he didn't know, and that that was not the sort of thing one could ask about in his family. In the Sixties he spoke frequently of the enthusiasm for Christian ideas – transfiguration, resurrection, preordained fate – he had acquired from his reading of Tolstoy and the New Testament, and most of all, I suppose, from the films of Dreyer and Bresson. He also admitted being impressed by the claim of the Indian spiritual leader Meher Baba that he was God or the Avatar. In later years, he seldom spoke of Christianity, but instead of Buddhism, especially in its Tibetan variety. In his last decades he amassed a large and valuable collection of Tibetan art and ritual objects.

Sometime after the founding of Anthology Film Archives, probably in the 1970s, Kelman gave at least two talks based on films in the Essential Cinema collection. The first was on Dreyer's *Gertrud* (1964), the other he called "Megafilm and Metafilm:" it was, in all likelihood, a distillation of the lectures from "Exercises in Film History." In 1973 he gave a lecture at the Carnegie Institute in Pittsburgh on *Gertrud*. Running through all of his lectures there is an appreciation of the insight of the great filmmakers into hitherto unexplored, or underexplored, potentials latent in a transfigural, life-giving art form.

The enormous value of his lectures derives from five aspects of Kelman's expositions: the clarity with which he selects and analyzes significant details, the originality of his insights (born of a nearly total indifference to previous critical and theoretical literature), his implicit view of cinema as the culmination of an ineluctable human aspiration to reproduce the image of Life and to conquer Death, his insistence on uniting realistic and magical tendencies (or rather, his belief that the illusion of reality is the highest achievement of magic), and the magisterial authority with which he isolates the individual achievement of each film artist, appreciating and molding what he imagines that artist under-stands to be a essential power of cinema.

Stanley Cavell.

Left to right: Ken Kelman, James Broughton, P. Adams Sitney, Jonas Mekas, Peter Kubelka.
(Photo: Stephen Shore).

Epilogue:
Confessions of a Film Historian

I refer to myself and to my experiences so often in the forgoing pages that this book has turned out to be a nearly autobiographical account of my cinematic taste and my engagement with films, filmmakers, and theoreticians. In truth, I never intended to become a film historian. The role was thrust upon me in my academic career. At first, I imagined I would earn my living as a professor of ancient Greek, later of Sanskrit.

When Arthur Knight's *The Liveliest Art* was published in 1957, the paperback edition was cheap enough for me to buy. As a high school student in New Haven, Connecticut, I tried to see as many of the films he mentioned as I might. That took me first to the Yale Film Society and then to founding the New Haven Film Society at the local YMCA, together with the painter, Jesse Epstein, the father of one of my friends, and my companion since childhood, George Landow.

Every week I read Jonas Mekas's "Movie Journal" in *The Village Voice*. At about the same time, I parlayed a job at the Yale-New Haven Hospital, testing rats and pigeons in Skinner boxes with LSD, into a visitor's card at Yale's Sterling library where I could read Jay Leyda's *Kino* (1958), Roger Manville's *Experiment in the Film* (1949), and Maya Deren's *Anagram of Ideas on Art, Form and Film* (1946).

I wrote the notes for the screenings of the New Haven Film Society, founding a journal called *Filmwise*, and pretentiously invited Mekas and other luminaries to submit essays. No one did until I met Stan Brakhage in 1961. He allowed me to print parts of his book-in-progress, *Metaphors on Vision*, in a special expanded edition of *Filmwise* to which Willard Maas, Parker Tyler, and Gregory Markopoulos were among the contributors. We subsequently put out special issues on Maya Deren, Gregory Markopoulos and finally, a double issue on Willard Maas and Marie Menken.

At that time, I was enthralled by Tyler's short essays in *Film Culture*, on Sidney Peterson, Willard Maas, Curtis Harrington, Charles Boultenhouse, and Markopoulos. I hoped someday to be able to write similar pieces defining the styles of other avant-garde filmmakers. I believe I succeeded thirty years later in my articles for *Artforum*. Some of them have been adapted into this book.

Odd Couples was influenced by the deliberately incongruous juxtapositions Sidney Peterson used in making his films. For instance, he put Picasso's etching, "Minotauramachie", together with Balzac's *Chef d'oeuvre inconnu,* and a Joycean monologue, spoken by a fictional model in an art school, to generate *Mr. Frenhofer and the Minotaur* (1948). Similarly, a diving suit and Old English ballads, transferred to Appalachia, became the bases for *The Lead Shoes* (1949).

In writing this Epilogue, I realized that I am also following the pattern of one of my favorite critical books: Erich Auerbach's *Mimesis*, where every chapter compares and contrasts two literary excerpts from the same period to chart the history of realism in Western literature. I had read the often-anthologized opening chapter, "Odysseus's Scar," on *The Odyssey* and Genesis as a teenager, but I didn't finish the book until much later, when I was more familiar with the Medieval and Renaissance texts that Auerbach particularly cared for. Once I realized how influential *Mimesis* had been for this book, I reread it and took from it the idea of an Epilogue instead of an Introduction.

By the time I finished high school, I was thoroughly familiar with the American avant-garde cinema and had published several articles. In those years I had befriended Ken Kelman, who was then a graduate student at the Yale Drama School. From him I learned of many of the filmmakers who would later preoccupy me, in particular Dreyer and Bresson. Jonas Mekas appointed me to direct the International Exposition of the New American Cinema in three manifestations (Europe 1963-64, Argentina 1965, and Europe again 1967-68). After that I taught for a year at Bard College, then NYU, while directing the Library and Publications of the newly formed Anthology Film Archives. Originally, Mekas had made me the general director of Anthology Film Archives, but I soon realized that I was unfit for the task.

At Bard College and at NYU's Cinema Studies Department I lectured on avant-garde cinema and gave seminars on film theory, the transition from silent to sound cinema, and on particular filmmakers – Dreyer, Brakhage, Bresson. I did not have responsibility for the whole history of cinema until I accepted a position at Princeton University in 1980. My second semester there I offered a course on Italian cinema that became the groundwork for my book, *Vital Crises in Italian Cinema*.

When I arrived at Princeton, I took over the format of a two-semester history of cinema course from my distinguished predecessor, Gilberto Perez. That entailed showing two approximately contemporary films each week. Thus, compelled to lecture on two different films every week for the thirty years I taught at Princeton, I worked out the bases of many of these chapters. But an invitation from the Cinemateca portuguesa in Lisbon was the proximate impetus of this book. In the final lecture of my five there, I came to see a closer linkage between Bergman's *Persona* and Tarkovsky's *Zerkalo* [*The Mirror*]. Once I got home, I wrote up what I had discovered in Lisbon. That reminded me of my Princeton lectures on Bergman's *Smiles of a Summer Night* and Dreyer's *Day of Wrath*. By the time I completed that chapter, the idea of a book of incongruous pairings took root in my brain. About half of the chapters resulted from combining and revising already published texts, and half were written expressly for this book.

Sometimes I would combine a revised older text with a new one. However, I have written on most of the films and filmmakers discussed here in my other books, articles, or encyclopedia entries. Whereas Auerbach discovered that the changing ideas of "Realism" and "Reality" had been his quarry throughout *Mimesis*, I could see only that cinematic style and its relationship to meaning unites the chapters of my study. Each chapter offered a distinct type of incongruity: centrality. verticality, montage, portraits of the artist, Aristophanic comedy, nearly contemporary examples of the evolution of film form, the use and misuse of psychoanalysis, national identity, opposed attitudes toward paintings, ironic filmmakers, cinematic recordings of private life, a filmmaker-gardener influenced by a filmmaker-farmer, and even contrasting theoreticians of Realism.

I arranged the book to start with two very different ways the silent cinema had of putting a character at the center of the screen. Charles Chaplin did it head-on, confident of his superior mimetic abilities to control the viewer's attention, but Carl Th. Dreyer used elaborate moving camera and the figure of a circle to give vibrancy to a filming of the trial of Joan of Arc, where little "action" took place. Joan occupies the center of the imaginary circle Dreyer created with his camera movements.

When Luis Buñuel and Salvador Dalí realized that montage favored the illusions of violence and even dismemberment, they wittily constructed *Un chien andalou* to demonstrate that, making in the process, the paradigmatic Surrealist film. Half a century later, David Lynch repeated that gesture, possibly aware of his magnificent precursors. However he is so reticent about his influences that one can merely speculate on the matter. Even though *Blue Velvet* seems to update and make explicit the sexuality of Hitchcock's *Rear Window*, a genetic connection, or influence, cannot be proven.

If, as I argue, comedy is a function of Dionysian religion, then religion – widely interpreted – would be a common thread in most of this book. But many readers would fail to credit the obscenities latent in *Bringing Up Baby* and overt in *There's Something About Mary* as vestiges of holiness. Likewise, the blasphemies of Dalí and Buñuel in both *Un chien andalou* and *L'age d'or* might not pass the scrutiny of some readers for religious images under negative or parodic signs.

Even more remotely, I take nationalism to be a religious notion in the 20th Century: thus, the films of Riefenstahl, Jennings, Mekas, Angelopoulos, and Hou exalt the homeland as divinely inspired and protected, as did the Soviet films I discussed in *Modernist Montage*. Finally, making art often borders on a religious vocation in the prime century of cinema. This has been especially true of the so-called avant-garde cinema, as exemplified here by the work of Buñuel, Dalí, Cocteau, Mekas, Brakhage, Hutton, Levine, Keller, Fisher, and Frampton. Even the last four, militant secularists, seem to recognize a transcendental aspect to making films. In this respect, I am appending here an email interview on the subject [slightly revised] I did with Sérgio Dias Branco in 2013 for *Cinema 4*'s special issue on "Cinema and Religion" in January 2013. Dias Branco's questions are in italics:

The film studies community know you mainly from your authoritative work on avant-garde cinema. Your work on religion and film is often forgotten or unknown, even if these strands are sometimes intertwined in your books on avant-garde films and filmmakers. How do you look at this split and connection as author and scholar?

It is reasonable that my writings on film and religion would be little known. I have written six books on cinema. Two of them, *Visionary Film: The American Avant-Garde* (1974, 1979, 2002) and *Eyes Upside Down: Visionary Filmmakers and the Heritage of Emerson* (2008) are explicitly studies of American avant-garde cinema. The other four, *Modernist Montage: The Obscurity of Vision in Cinema and Literature* (1992), *Vital Crises in Italian Cinema: Iconography, Stylistics, Politics* (1995, 2013), *The Cinema of Poetry* (2015) and *Marvelous Names in Literature and Cinema* (2023) touch occasionally on aspects of religion (i.e., Dreyer, Bresson, Rossellini, Fellini, Olmi, Pasolini, Hitchcock. Tarkovsky, Cornell, Dorsky) but never as a thematic thread to delineate the chapters of a book. My essays on religion in the work of Scorsese, Allen, and my general essay for Eliade's *Encyclopedia of Religion* (1987) were written intermittently over thirty years and have not been collected in a single volume before this. Therefore, that persistent strain in my writing might well escape attention.

Furthermore, the aspects of religion that I discuss in my writings on avant-garde cinema are never the center of an exegesis. They do not even treat conventional aspects of religion, as understood in cinema studies. For instance, Maya Deren's concern with ritual and Voodoo, Kenneth Anger's Satanism, Stan Brakhage's Emersonian stance, Larry Jordan's mysticism, Joseph Cornell's allegiance to Christian Science and Nathaniel Dorsky's concept of filmic devotions are all functions of their aesthetics, and in differing degrees are latent in their films. I touch on them in passing while concentrating on their cinematic inventions and the evolution of their film styles. The earlier avant-gardes, in France and the Soviet Union, were explicitly anti-religious or deliberately blasphemous. Consequently, my discussions of their works do not fall within the usual rubrics of religious studies.

At Princeton University, you have been involved in the research project Cinema and Religious Expression, sponsored by the Center for the Study of Religion, which you co-directed with Jeffrey Stout. Also with Stout, you have taught a course on religion and cinema. Can you talk about the approach, scope, and aim of this project and this course?

At Princeton University, like many of the professors who teach Religion, Stout does not profess a faith. I, however, am a practicing Roman Catholic and an oddball one at that: liberal in matters of morals, but liturgically ultraconservative. Our personal religious views play absolutely no role in the course we gave together. We have congruous tastes in film: Brakhage, Dreyer, Kurosawa, Bergman, Tarkovsky, Bresson, Landow, Dorsky, etc. are shared enthusiasms. Both of Stout's sons, Noah and Livingston, were filmmakers. His participation in their education and early careers played a funda-mental role in the formation of his views of cinema.

It was very easy for us to agree upon a syllabus. Our readings included Kierkegaard, Tarkovsky, New Testament, Girard, Santayana, Bresson, Bernanos, O'Connor, Nietzsche, Augustine, and Emerson. Your readers, or European audiences in general, might not realize that the aesthetics of American artists have been massively dominated by often contradictory aspects of Emerson's philosophy. One might even say that Emerson brought into focus a native American religion of "self-reliance" and "experience" (his terms) to which most of our artists, even atheists, have subscribed, often without realizing it. Stout is an authority on Emerson. As such he was later of enormous help to me when I wrote *Eyes Upside Down*. In turn, I believe I have been influential on his understanding of the technical and formal aspects of cinema. After we taught a course together in 2000-2001, he has continued to teach Cinema and Religion on his own. In 2007 he gave the Stone Lectures at the Princeton Theological Seminary: "A Light That Shines in the Darkness: Evil, Egotism, and the Sacred in Film," which will appear as a book.

Let me pick up on the importance that you, as a Christian, attach to liturgy. Has your aesthetic immersion in religion impacted on your study of film? Have you ever been interested in the field of theological aesthetics? I am also thinking about the connections between the poetic, often lyrical, writings of mystics like John of the Cross and the work of avant-garde filmmakers like Bruce Baillie.

Although I do not see offhand a relationship between St. John of the Cross and Baillie, I would be eager to read an essay on that subject if you have one. I am too literal-minded to make that leap myself. I do discuss St. John of the Cross when I lecture on the Straub/Huillet film, *Der Bräutigam, die Komödiantin und der Zuhälter* (*The Bridegroom, the Actress and the Pimp*, 1968) because they cite his poetry in the film. Generally, I do not find analogical criticism particularly useful. I want to know what the filmmakers were reading and thinking and how their sources shaped their films. With considerable caution one might want to extend those sources to forces active in the filmmakers' culture. I did that when I repeatedly invoked passages from Dante in analyzing films in *Vital Crises in Italian Cinema* or Emerson and Whitman in *Eyes Upside Down*. But I would not bring up Emerson or Whitman in discussing an Italian filmmaker unless I had evidence that he or she had read either of them, nor Dante for an American avant-garde filmmaker without similar evidence.

Of course, my liturgical worship and my theological readings have influenced my film criticism, but so has my examination of Protestant writings, ancient Greek religion, Stoic and Epicurean philosophy, Nietzsche, Heidegger, etc. I will grasp at anything that throws light on the films that occupy my mind. I am not sure what you mean by "theological aesthetics." I assumed that all aesthetics had theological implications. I have never consciously explored that domain as an academic discipline.

I was not suggesting a direct connection between John of the Cross's writings and Baillie's films – although perhaps I could do it in regard to David Lynch's films… – but merely pointing out that they can both be seen as lyrical poets. Catholic film thinkers such as André Bazin and Robert Bresson have been interested in discussing the role of reality in cinematographic art, even though their reflections are not identical since they come from different perspectives and reach different conclusions.

You are more concerned with artistic ideas and expression embodied in film. Do you regard these differences as subjective, connected with different ways of understanding and experiencing the Catholic faith (understandings and experiences fostered by catholicity and the way it points towards ecumenism)? Or do you think that this aspect is irrelevant, and we are just talking about three distinct film thinkers who also happen to be Catholic?

I am tempted to answer that these are just three distinct film thinkers who happen to be Catholics, but for two important points. In the first place, it would be absurd for me to put myself in a class with Bazin and Bresson. More to the point, however, is the fact that I find the question fascinating and provocative. I have not felt the influence of Bazin in my work. In fact, I think my concentration on the Romantic tradition and the function of the imagination in cinema has been, if anything, anti-Bazinian. But I have been greatly influenced by René Girard, a Catholic scholar of literature (never on film) who has devoted his very distinguished career to aspects of literary realism and its relation to Truth.

Therefore, your question makes me somewhat uncomfortably aware of the "Protestant" bias of my aesthetics. In this I am not alone, as an American. Even our greatest Catholic fiction writer, Flannery O'Connor, chooses radical Southern Protestants for her subjects. Catholic thought has had little effect on the arts in America. My own aesthetic formation emerged from reading ancient Greek and Roman writers – with a Nietzschean emphasis on ritual – and from a thorough immersion in the English-language Romantics, Blake and Wordsworth, whom I adored; they may have been nominally Christians; Emerson and Melville perhaps not even that, but none of them had any use for the Roman Catholic Church.

Jean-Luc Godard once said "I'm not a religious person, but I'm a faithful person. I believe in images." This opens the door for a discussion that goes beyond works of art with religious subjects, which of course may be rich and complex. What are your thoughts about the connection between faith and visual art, particularly in film?

Gilles Deleuze, apparently elaborating on Godard's point, makes the more lucid case that we (and the modern cinema) no longer believe in the world. He understands this as a transformation of what he posits as the affinity between cinema and Catholicism. In fact, he cites Godard's cinema as precisely the locus where belief in the world is most decisively at stake. I find Deleuze's notion fascinating. However, I do not see any relationship at all between the theological virtue of faith – the gift that convinces me that God is in Three Persons, for example, or that I am subject to an infinity of hell or heaven – and cinema, which can astound me, move me to tears, thrill me, bore me or disgust me, but can convince me of nothing. In short,

ODD COUPLES + 236

visual art can evoke or merely refer to theological revelations, but it cannot conjure or even reenforce faith.

What do you see as the prospects for the scholarly interaction between cinema, philosophy, and religion?

There is already a fecund interrelationship between philosophy and film studies. I am thinking particularly of the writings on film by Gilles Deleuze and Stanley Cavell. As far as I know, there is nothing of comparable sophistication on religion and cinema, unless it would be the yet unpublished work of Jeffrey Stout.

Such an interaction will always depend on the work of filmmakers and the elements that they use and evoke – like the Christian components in some of Stan Brakhage's films. Are there any recent films that have made you think philosophically and religiously about them?

Die große Stille (*Into Great Silence*, 2005) and the recently unveiled films of Jerome Hiler (made over the last fifty years) touch upon religious issues, very obviously. However, I would not ever claim to "think philosophically and religiously." I am merely a film historian. By the way, as a film historian, I find the "Christian components" in Brakhage's later films of minimal interest, even in regard to what I consider the religious strain in his work.

In conclusion, I hope this is my last book. When I retired from teaching in 2015, I promised myself to read through all of Plato in ancient Greek and to abandon cinema. I stopped going to films because of my dislike of looking at digital images. I had read through most of Plato when the Covid epidemic confined me to my Rhode Island house for a year. In that time, I completed Plato and read through all of the ancient Greek dramas with the help of numerous commentaries. I also wrote two new books and edited Ken Kelman's lectures and film writings. The first of those books, *Marvelous Names in Literature and Cinema* has been published by Crescent Moon as I was finishing this book, which they will also publish. The Kelman book will come from Anthology Film Archives. My other book of 2019, *Brakhage, Straub/ Huillet, Deleuze and the Philosophy of Modern Cinema*, will be a Crescent Moon book.

CRESCENT MOON PUBLISHING

web: www.crmoon.com e-mail: cresmopub@yahoo.co.uk

ARTS, PAINTING, SCULPTURE

The Art of Andy Goldsworthy
Andy Goldsworthy: Touching Nature
Andy Goldsworthy in Close-Up
Andy Goldsworthy: Pocket Guide
Andy Goldsworthy In America
Land Art: A Complete Guide
The Art of Richard Long
Richard Long: Pocket Guide
Land Art In the UK
Land Art in Close-Up
Land Art In the U.S.A.
Land Art: Pocket Guide
Installation Art in Close-Up
Minimal Art and Artists In the 1960s and After
Colourfield Painting
Land Art DVD, TV documentary
Andy Goldsworthy DVD, TV documentary
The Erotic Object: Sexuality in Sculpture From Prehistory to the Present Day
Sex in Art: Pornography and Pleasure in Painting and Sculpture
Postwar Art
Sacred Gardens: The Garden in Myth, Religion and Art
Glorification: Religious Abstraction in Renaissance and 20th Century Art
Early Netherlandish Painting
Leonardo da Vinci
Piero della Francesca
Giovanni Bellini
Fra Angelico: Art and Religion in the Renaissance
Mark Rothko: The Art of Transcendence
Frank Stella: American Abstract Artist
Jasper Johns
Brice Marden
Alison Wilding: The Embrace of Sculpture
Vincent van Gogh: Visionary Landscapes
Eric Gill: Nuptials of God
Constantin Brancusi: Sculpting the Essence of Things
Max Beckmann
Caravaggio
Gustave Moreau
Egon Schiele: Sex and Death In Purple Stockings
Delizioso Fotografico Fervore: Works In Process 1
Sacro Cuore: Works In Process 2
The Light Eternal: J.M.W. Turner
The Madonna Glorified: Karen Arthurs

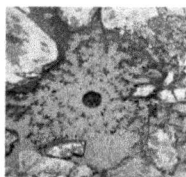

LITERATURE

J.R.R. Tolkien: The Books, The Films, The Whole Cultural Phenomenon
J.R.R. Tolkien: Pocket Guide
Tolkien's Heroic Quest
The *Earthsea* Books of Ursula Le Guin
Beauties, Beasts and Enchantment: Classic French Fairy Tales
German Popular Stories by the Brothers Grimm
Philip Pullman and *His Dark Materials*
Sexing Hardy: Thomas Hardy and Feminism
Thomas Hardy's *Tess of the d'Urbervilles*
Thomas Hardy's *Jude the Obscure*
Thomas Hardy: The Tragic Novels
Love and Tragedy: Thomas Hardy
The Poetry of Landscape in Hardy
Wessex Revisited: Thomas Hardy and John Cowper Powys
Wolfgang Iser: Essays and Interviews
Petrarch, Dante and the Troubadours
Maurice Sendak and the Art of Children's Book Illustration
Andrea Dworkin
Cixous, Irigaray, Kristeva: The *Jouissance* of French Feminism
Julia Kristeva: Art, Love, Melancholy, Philosophy, Semiotics and Psychoanalysis
Hélène Cixous I Love You: The *Jouissance* of Writing
Luce Irigaray: Lips, Kissing, and the Politics of Sexual Difference
Peter Redgrove: Here Comes the Flood
Peter Redgrove: Sex-Magic-Poetry-Cornwall
Lawrence Durrell: Between Love and Death, East and West
Love, Culture & Poetry: Lawrence Durrell
Cavafy: Anatomy of a Soul
German Romantic Poetry: Goethe, Novalis, Heine, Hölderlin
Feminism and Shakespeare
Shakespeare: Love, Poetry & Magic
The Passion of D.H. Lawrence
D.H. Lawrence: Symbolic Landscapes
D.H. Lawrence: Infinite Sensual Violence
Rimbaud: Arthur Rimbaud and the Magic of Poetry
The Ecstasies of John Cowper Powys
Sensualism and Mythology: The Wessex Novels of John Cowper Powys
Amorous Life: John Cowper Powys and the Manifestation of Affectivity (H.W. Fawkner)
Postmodern Powys: New Essays on John Cowper Powys (Joe Boulter)
Rethinking Powys: Critical Essays on John Cowper Powys
Paul Bowles & Bernardo Bertolucci
Rainer Maria Rilke
Joseph Conrad: *Heart of Darkness*
In the Dim Void: Samuel Beckett
Samuel Beckett Goes into the Silence
André Gide: Fiction and Fervour
Jackie Collins and the Blockbuster Novel
Blinded By Her Light: The Love-Poetry of Robert Graves
The Passion of Colours: Travels In Mediterranean Lands
Poetic Forms

POETRY

Ursula Le Guin: Walking In Cornwall
Peter Redgrove: Here Comes The Flood
Peter Redgrove: Sex-Magic-Poetry-Cornwall
Dante: Selections From the Vita Nuova
Petrarch, Dante and the Troubadours
William Shakespeare: Sonnets
William Shakespeare: Complete Poems
Blinded By Her Light: The Love-Poetry of Robert Graves
Emily Dickinson: Selected Poems
Emily Brontë: Poems
Thomas Hardy: Selected Poems
Percy Bysshe Shelley: Poems
John Keats: Selected Poems
Joh n Keats: Poems of 1820
D.H. Lawrence: Selected Poems
Edmund Spenser: Poems
Edmund Spenser: Amoretti
John Donne: Poems
Henry Vaughan: Poems
Sir Thomas Wyatt: Poems
Robert Herrick: Selected Poems
Rilke: Space, Essence and Angels in the Poetry of Rainer Maria Rilke
Rainer Maria Rilke: Selected Poems
Friedrich Hölderlin: Selected Poems
Arseny Tarkovsky: Selected Poems
Arthur Rimbaud: Selected Poems
Arthur Rimbaud: A Season in Hell
Arthur Rimbaud and the Magic of Poetry
Novalis: Hymns To the Night
German Romantic Poetry
Paul Verlaine: Selected Poems
Elizaethan Sonnet Cycles
D.J. Enright: By-Blows
Jeremy Reed: Brigitte's Blue Heart
Jeremy Reed: Claudia Schiffer's Red Shoes
Gorgeous Little Orpheus
Radiance: New Poems
Crescent Moon Book of Nature Poetry
Crescent Moon Book of Love Poetry
Crescent Moon Book of Mystical Poetry
Crescent Moon Book of Elizabethan Love Poetry
Crescent Moon Book of Metaphysical Poetry
Crescent Moon Book of Romantic Poetry
Pagan America: New American Poetry

MEDIA, CINEMA, FEMINISM and CULTURAL STUDIES

J.R.R. Tolkien: The Books, The Films, The Whole Cultural Phenomenon
J.R.R. Tolkien: Pocket Guide
The *Lord of the Rings* Movies: Pocket Guide
The Cinema of Hayao Miyazaki
Hayao Miyazaki: *Princess Mononoke*: Pocket Movie Guide
Hayao Miyazaki: *Spirited Away*: Pocket Movie Guide
Tim Burton : Hallowe'en For Hollywood
Ken Russell
Ken Russell: *Tommy*: Pocket Movie Guide
The Ghost Dance: The Origins of Religion
The Peyote Cult
Cixous, Irigaray, Kristeva: The *Jouissance* of French Feminism
Julia Kristeva: Art, Love, Melancholy, Philosophy, Semiotics and Psychoanalysis
Luce Irigaray: Lips, Kissing, and the Politics of Sexual Difference
Hélene Cixous I Love You: The *Jouissance* of Writing
Andrea Dworkin
'Cosmo Woman': The World of Women's Magazines
Women in Pop Music
HomeGround: The Kate Bush Anthology
Discovering the Goddess (Geoffrey Ashe)
The Poetry of Cinema
The Sacred Cinema of Andrei Tarkovsky
Andrei Tarkovsky: Pocket Guide
Andrei Tarkovsky: *Mirror*: Pocket Movie Guide
Andrei Tarkovsky: *The Sacrifice*: Pocket Movie Guide
Walerian Borowczyk: Cinema of Erotic Dreams
Jean-Luc Godard: The Passion of Cinema
Jean-Luc Godard: *Hail Mary*: Pocket Movie Guide
Jean-Luc Godard: *Contempt*: Pocket Movie Guide
Jean-Luc Godard: *Pierrot le Fou*: Pocket Movie Guide
John Hughes and Eighties Cinema
Ferris Bueller's Day Off: Pocket Movie Guide
Jean-Luc Godard: Pocket Guide
The Cinema of Richard Linklater
Liv Tyler: Star In Ascendance
Blade Runner and the Films of Philip K. Dick
Paul Bowles and Bernardo Bertolucci
Media Hell: Radio, TV and the Press
An Open Letter to the BBC
Detonation Britain: Nuclear War in the UK
Feminism and Shakespeare
Wild Zones: Pornography, Art and Feminism
Sex in Art: Pornography and Pleasure in Painting and Sculpture
Sexing Hardy: Thomas Hardy and Feminism

The Light Eternal is a model monograph, an exemplary job. The subject matter of the book is beautifully organised and dead on beam. (Lawrence Durrell)
It is amazing for me to see my work treated with such passion and respect. (Andrea Dworkin)

CRESCENT MOON PUBLISHING
P.O. Box 1312, Maidstone, Kent, ME14 5XU, Great Britain. www.crmoon.com

cresmopub@yahoo.co.uk   www.crescentmoon.org.uk